Praise for *It's Not About You—It's About God*

"Through practical illustrations women will identify with the struggle of allowing God to operate on their lives. Although women may say 'Ouch' while Rebecca is used as an instrument in the hand of God to perform much-needed surgery on deep heart issues, they will also say 'Thank God' as she applies the balm of Gilead."

SABRINA D. BLACK, author of *Can Two Walk Together? Prone to Wander* and *HELP! for Your Leadership*

Praise for *Chosen Vessels*

"I believe this book will be a tremendous blessing and source of inspiration for all who read it."

DR. MYLES MUNROE, author of *Understanding the Purpose and Power of Women*

"Chosen Vessels gripped my heart like no other book. . . . This book brings women face to face with commonsense, biblical answers for breaking free from cultural, racial and religious bondage."

CAROL KENT, speaker and author of *Becoming a Woman of Influence*

"Rebecca Osaigbovo has broken the long silence of African American women. . . . In *Chosen Vessels* we hear a voice from the inside. . . . In this book Rebecca provides a road other women can follow in helping to restore the black family to a biblical foundation."

From the foreword by DR. JOHN M. PERKINS

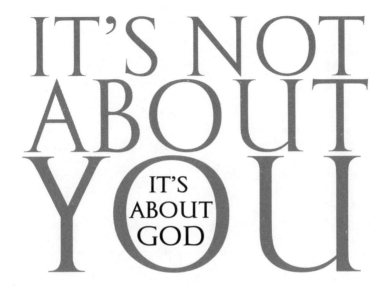

IT'S NOT ABOUT YOU IT'S ABOUT GOD

Rebecca Florence Osaigbovo

IVP Books

An imprint of InterVarsity Press
Downers Grove, Illinois

InterVarsity Press
P.O. Box 1400, Downers Grove, IL 60515-1426
World Wide Web: www.ivpress.com
E-mail: mail@ivpress.com

InterVarsity Press® is the book-publishing division of InterVarsity Christian Fellowship/USA®, a student movement active on campus at hundreds of universities, colleges and schools of nursing in the United States of America, and a member movement of the International Fellowship of Evangelical Students. For information about local and regional activities, write Public Relations Dept., InterVarsity Christian Fellowship/USA, 6400 Schroeder Rd., P.O. Box 7895, Madison, WI 53707-7895, or visit the IVCF website at <www.intervarsity.org>.

All Scripture quotations, unless otherwise indicated, are taken from the New King James Version. *Copyright © 1982 by Thomas Nelson, Inc. Used by permission. All rights reserved.*

"The Thing That Cannot Happen" and "My Name Is Joseph" were originally published in A Diary of Joseph *by Diane Proctor Reeder. Copyright © 2000. Used by permission.*

Design: Cindy Kiple

Images: Ryan McVay/Getty Images

ISBN-10: 0-8308-2367-0
ISBN-13: 978-0-8308-2367-3

Printed in the United States of America ∞

Library of Congress Cataloging-in-Publication Data

Osaigbovo, Rebecca.
 It's not about you—it's about God/Rebecca Florence Osaigbovo.
  p. cm.
 ISBN 9-8308-2367-0 (pbk.: alk. paper)
 1. African American women—Religious life. I. Title.
 BR563.N4O835 2004
 248.8'43—dc22

                                                                          2003018833

P	23	22	21	20	19	18	17	16	15	14	13	12	11	10	9		
Y	21	20	19	18	17	16	15	14	13	12	11	10	09	08	07	06	

This book is dedicated to
my most significant other (after the Lord Jesus Christ)—
Uwaifo Francis Osaigbovo,
who just celebrated a half-century of living
(happy birthday, sweetheart!)
and twenty-five years of being married to me.
Now that deserves a special reward.

To contact Rebecca Osaigbovo regarding her speaking ministry write

Chosen Vessels Ministries
P.O. Box 23872
Detroit, MI 48223
Rfosaigbovo@aol.com
313/531-7534
www.cvmi.org

CONTENTS

Part one

WHO'S IN CHARGE HERE?

1

I Didn't Ask for This

In September of my senior year in high school—after thinking about it, debating over it and counting the cost—at last I had done it. I had finally decided I could trust God to control my life. After months of God dealing with my heart, I was drawn to give my life over to him unconditionally.

I was in the prime of my life and things could not have been better. I had made the all-regional basketball team the year before. I was a national merit scholar, qualified to test for scholarships. I had done well on my college entrance exams, and I was on my way to the big city (Chicago) to go to college. But something intervened.

About a month, maybe six weeks, after making the decision to completely sell out to God, I ended up in the hospital with a rare blood disease that is usually fatal. I went from being a healthy basketball player to someone who was knocking on death's door. The door opened and I almost got sucked in.

I went into a coma, had numerous blood transfusions, underwent several surgeries and suffered partial paralysis. At one point, the doctors told my parents that I was unlikely to survive an emergency spleendectomy, but if I did live, I would be a vegetable.

After two months in the hospital, including an extensive stay in ICU, I was discharged on Christmas Eve. But I had to go back to the hospital in February for more surgery. Sometime in March, when I attempted to return to school, I found out I was too weak to stay in school all day and too far behind to catch up. In the spring of what was supposed to be my last year in high school, I was at home recuperating, with a lot of time on my hands to think about what had happened in the last six months. I was trying to make sense of things. But to be honest, I was more than a little confused.

My life had taken a drastic turn, and I wondered about many things. Would I have to stay in high school another year and graduate with my younger brother's class? Why did I have to miss out on playing basketball during my senior year? Why in the world did I have to be sick at the time I was supposed to take a test to qualify for college scholarships? Why did the young man who was in the hospital at the same time I was die and I live? But the biggest question on my mind was: Why would God allow me to experience so much pain and disappointment? Why did he let these unexpected circumstances happen in my life, especially when I had just given him my all?

I was really bothered. You would think if you gave Christ your life unconditionally, he would take much better care of you. As I tried to understand God and figure out how and why these things had happened, I got so discouraged that I became depressed. I seriously began to wonder if God was really all I had been taught. Was he really good? Was he really bigger than the devil? It surely did not appear so. Did God really know what he was doing? Did he know how to take care of me? What possible good could come out of the recent events in my life? How could this experience possibly benefit me?

ME, ME, ME

Most of us interpret the things of God with a self-centered perspective. For too long, we have put too much emphasis on me, me, me. However, to be in God's kingdom means to be governed by God's ways. God's way of thinking is on a higher level than ours (Isaiah 55:8-9).

At the age of seventeen, I could not figure out how anything good could come from my bad situation. I looked at life with God from the perspective of what I could get out of him, not what he could get out of me. That's why I could not understand why a sovereign God would allow my life to be turned upside down right after I had told him he could do anything in and through my life. Yet I had told him in my unconditional surrender that he could have all of me, without reservation.

Upon hearing of my physical plight, the local paper interviewed my mother. They asked what people could do for us, thinking she would surely ask for money to help with the medical bills that were piling up. (As faith missionaries, my family had no health insurance.) Instead, my mother asked for prayer. The Associated Press picked up the story and the request for prayer went out across the country. I received cards from people all over saying they were praying for me.

In the early seventies, the story of my illness and the request for prayer brought people together across racial lines in a small southern town and around the country. God's miraculous healing lifted many people's faith in God and in prayer. Even the physicians at the university hospital had to admit that God was involved. The day I was discharged, one of the doctors told me I was a miracle but he hoped he had contributed at least a little to my recovery.

Now as I look back I can see that much good has been the result. That experience laid a foundation in my life for confidence in the possibilities of prayer. Another benefit is I don't fear death. I know God brought me from death's door because he had a work for me to do. I know I won't leave here until the work is finished.

I credit God with the fact that I was allowed to go to college without graduating from high school. I had received my admission letter while I was in the hospital. The school decided to let me enter based on my test scores and my record through my junior year.

Since my senior year in high school, I have had a variety of disappointing, difficult and painful experiences. I don't claim to understand everything, but today I believe I have a much better handle on the "whys" of what I experienced that year and since then. I have asked God some hard questions. In fact, I think God put questions in me because he wanted to answer them. He has given me the answer to many of my questions. The answer is that it's not about me. It's about God.

How did I come to that conclusion? There was no single experience that gave me that answer. Because of the questions God placed in my heart, I have looked for answers. As a result, he has changed the way I think about myself, about him and about life. I have learned that when you give your life unconditionally to God, your life no longer revolves around you. From that point on, it's all about God.

A GOD-CENTERED PERSPECTIVE

I have found that most of my difficulties or frustrations in life have been due to a faulty premise and wrong thinking. As these lies have been exposed, I have come into greater degrees of freedom. The truth of God's Word has been setting me free. It is a process. The most difficult part of the journey thus far has been discovering that much of what I believed and had been taught about the purpose of my relationship with God was wrong.

When most of us give our lives to God, our biggest consideration is what we will receive. Sermons that draw us to God are those that tell us how we can escape hell and live for eternity in heaven, walking on streets of gold. Teachings that keep us with God are laden with promises of health, peace, success, happiness, prosperity and the answers to all our problems.

Well, I'm not going to burst your bubble. I believe all of the above and more are true. However, if that's all you desire in life, you need look no further. And if you're like some people I know, perhaps you are bored with the status quo. Maybe you're ready to put down your toys; you're ready for adventure; you're ready for some challenges that will force you to grow. God is drawing you to a greater purpose. Possibly you're ready to see not what you can get out of God but what God can get out of you.

God is giving you an invitation to purposely live your life on a higher plane. He desires your permission to demonstrate his ways through your life. If you do say yes to his invitation, know up front that no matter what you have gone through and may yet go through, it really is not about you. I wish I had known this truth back when I struggled trying to figure out why my life had been turned upside down.

"Think outside the box" is a phrase people often use today. To be the women God desires to use, it is imperative that we see, think and act beyond what we know or think we know. We cannot afford to focus on what seems apparent. We cannot afford to look at life from a self-centered perspective. We need to begin to understand life from God's perspective. We must see everything in life, including our identity, in relationship to God, the center of the universe.

The purposes and plans of God are spiritual realities that exist beneath the surface. We will experience frustration, delay God's plans and maybe even disqualify ourselves from his use if our eyes remain closed to those realities. We must realize that what we see and think is far from reality and the things that really matter.

If our lives are truly his and we truly want to benefit from all he is in us and through us, we definitely need to readjust our focus and reestablish our priorities. We say God is number one. Let's make him that in reality, not just in words. To do this, many African American Christian women will have to make major changes. The center of the universe calls us to deny ourselves. Sometimes we must choose his way instead of the way we have always done it before. We may have to choose his thinking on the matter rather than the thinking that is inherent in our culture or that is traditional to black females.

WHY THIS BOOK?

We could live our whole existence trapped in the earthly, thinking that life consists only of what is seen, living by what we understand in the natural. We could be good Christians, claiming all of the promises of the Word, and still miss out on really living.

Fortunately, some of you are sensing there is something much bigger. There's a nagging thought in the back of your mind that there has got to be something more than this. God is calling you to a perspective that is out of this world. If you accept the premise that it is not about you, I'll guarantee when you begin to discover what and who it is all about, you will not be disappointed.

When we know it's not about us but about God and his purposes, our circumstances and even our challenges take on a whole different look. As we move from our ways of understanding to his way of thinking, we move into higher realms of being. We move beyond the seen to the unseen. We move above circumstances. We move into freedom.

The goal of this book is to liberate women to move forward into spiritual maturity. We need to be liberated in our mind. What we think about our identity may be our worst prison. We need to be liberated from the traditions of men that make the Word of God ineffective (Mark 7:13). The primary liberation we need is from a self-centered existence, the idea that it's all about us.

We will also look at God's dealings with people such as Job, Moses, Joseph, the servant of Elijah, Gideon and other biblical characters who found that events in their lives were about things much bigger than themselves. To fulfill the destiny God had called them to, they had to abandon the self-centered point of view. They had to realize that God's way of thinking was not the same as their way. Some of them also found that there was more to life than the things seen with the natural eye.

Throughout this book, we will come back to a few points over and over:

- There is an unseen scene behind the seen.
- Much of what happens in the seen realm has significance in the unseen.
- God desires that his people be co-laborers with him to make a statement to the unseen evil world.
- When we take our focus off ourselves, we are better equipped to become partners with God.
- God's ways are completely different from—and sometimes the opposite of—ours.
- It is essential for us to come up to God's ways in our attitudes and actions.

As you learn to apply these points, you will also find answers about experiences you have personally encountered. As you think about your life from a God-centered perspective, I trust that you will also conclude that it is not about you and wake up to the purposes God has for you. As you adjust your perspective, I believe you will come away with a new hope in a God who truly loves you. As you become more acutely aware of what God may desire to say through your life to the unseen realm, I pray that you will be more determined to trust God unconditionally.

CONCLUSIONS

I write this book as part of a mandate to God's call on my life to tear down, throw down, root out and destroy those things that hinder his perfect will in the lives of his people, especially women (Jeremiah 1:10). Likewise, I desire to build and plant the purpose of God that we might be used as co-laborers with God in bringing into manifestation the defeat of Satan's work that Christ already secured on the cross.

Some conclusions in this book have come from wrestling with God, who stretched me (and is still stretching me) as we wrestled. As you read, your thinking will also be stretched. I still have questions; I don't have all of the answers. But I can share with you what I have discovered thus far.

I warn you that some of these things may be a departure from traditional thinking. I have to admit that I have rarely been one to think along traditional lines. However, I'm not asking you to blindly accept my conclusions without question or scrutiny. We don't need to give anyone the power of thinking for us.

Please be as diligent as the Bereans were when they heard the apostle Paul (Acts 17:11). Don't simply take my word for it. See if what I say is in accordance with the Word of God. If it is not, then don't accept it. In the body of Christ, we need people who think independently of the crowd, whose thoughts line up with God's ways and his Word. Much of what we believe is based on what we have been taught. Because we trust those who teach us, we rarely question the content and, even less often, study for ourselves. So don't take my word for it. But don't take what you have always believed as truth either.

As you read, just know this: It's really not about you.

The Myth of the Strong Black Christian Woman

When I was speaking to a group of African American women in Nashville, Tennessee, I said, "You know as black women, we've had to be strong. We've been the ones to hold our families together. If it wasn't for us, our families would be in worse shape than they are in right now." I got all kinds of nods and amens.

Then I talked about the fact that God is not interested in strong black *Christian* women. "Hmmm." At first, the idea took this audience by surprise, but when I explained to them what I'm going to say in this chapter, the light hit them, as it has hit others since that time. Everywhere that I speak on this, women have expressed their appreciation after being challenged with this new idea.

Too often we use the term "strong black woman" in a prideful way, taking credit for what we have been in our families and communities. That is why we nod our heads, sigh and have tears come to our eyes as we contemplate all we have been through and the fact that we are still standing. We think of the struggles we've experienced in getting our children through school, dealing with absent fathers, collecting child support, opposing the prison system, paying the rent, finding transportation, working with the racist boss. Some of us have had in-law problems. At times we've struggled to get food on the table. When our husbands or sons and daughters have been addicted to alcohol or crack, we've held the family together, sometimes working two jobs. We've gone without so the kids can get school supplies or those $150 tennis shoes they just *had* to have. The strong black woman appears to be alive and well. We have survived.

I don't deny that we, as black women, have gone through more than our share of holding things together in our families and communities, even in our churches. I will not deny that many of us claim to be Christians. At face value, we really could take a lot of credit for what we have overcome and accomplished in spite of the obstacles. But I think we really need to be careful to whom we credit our strength. When we take the credit, we are not giving it to God. Our purpose as Christians is to give the credit and glory to God.

In saying this, I want to be careful not to take anything away from our history and the abundant examples of women who have stood in the midst of adversity and still gotten over. I applaud the thousands of black women who in years gone by have paved the way for me.

I'M A PRODUCT OF A STRONG BLACK WOMAN

My grandmother was one of many women who sacrificed so that their children could go to college and have a better life than they had. Some of these women, like my grandmother, accomplished these tasks without the help of fully functioning husbands—if they had husbands at all.

My grandmother worked as a domestic. When my mom was born, she realized she did not want to raise a child in her current environment with an alcoholic husband. She decided to leave her husband and raise my mother on her own, with the help of her mother. She did it, making sacrifices to eventually send my mother from St. Louis to Detroit to live with relatives and attend Wayne State University in the 1940s.

My mother became a believer through InterVarsity Christian Fellowship as a senior at Wayne State. She went on to Bible school, married my father and served with him as a missionary in Tennessee at Cedine Bible Mission until she went home to be with the Lord in 1995. My father chronicles their lives as African American missionaries in the book *Faith Flows in Ebony*.

My grandmother came to live with us, and she also became a Christian. She went home to be with the Lord when I was five. Though I do not remember a lot about her, I loved my grandmother. She was very special to me. She took an interest in me. I was a middle child in a family of five children at the time of her death, and she had a great impact on me for the short time I experienced her life.

Although my grandmother did not become a Christian until later in life, I still believe God's hand was always on her. I give God the credit for the strength she had to accomplish in her early life what must have been very difficult for her.

But my mother and grandmother didn't do this by their own strength. Instead, they recognized their weakness and leaned heavily on God, with faith that he could bear their weight. God wants to be the strength of the Christian African American woman's life. The only way he can be our strength is for us to be weak.

The notion of a strong black *Christian* woman is a myth. It's not that we cannot be strong. The question is, from whence comes our strength? The Word of God tells us, "Be strong in the Lord and in the power of his might" (Ephesians 6:10). God wants us to be strong, but the strength of God is a little unusual. His strength is not manifested in our lives through our own strength. God's strength is made evident as we are weak (2 Corinthians 12:9).

UNDERSTANDING THE WAYS OF GOD

If we understood the ways of God, then we would not get so upset when stuff happens or when things don't go the way we want them to. The apostle Paul understood the ways of God. We see that in 2 Corinthians chapter 12:

> And lest I should be exalted above measure by the abundance of the revelations, a thorn in the flesh was given to me, a messenger of Satan to buffet me, lest I be exalted above measure. Concerning this thing I pleaded with the Lord three times that it might depart from me. And He said to me, "My grace is sufficient for you, for My strength is made perfect in weakness." Therefore most gladly I will rather boast in my infirmities, that the power of Christ may rest upon me. Therefore I take pleasure in infirmities, in reproaches, in needs, in persecutions, in distresses, for Christ's sake. For when I am weak, then I am strong. (2 Corinthians 12:7-10)

Paul was having some trouble; he was having a situation in his life that he didn't like. He tells us he had a messenger sent from hell. Some of us think our bosses or spouses are messengers from hell. Paul says he pleaded with the Lord three times that the thorn in his flesh might depart from him. It was very tight for Paul. He didn't like what was happening; he didn't like this messenger of Satan buffeting him. And he went to God three times saying, "Oh God, please God, take this away from me."

Paul did what most of us have done. We plead with God to remove the unpleasant things from our lives. Many of us don't stop asking after three times. After three hundred times, we're still begging, "God, take him away from me; take her away from me; take this drama away from me; take this situation away from me." We've pleaded with God, "Please, take it away. It's uncomfortable. I don't like it." It may be a job, a marriage, a daughter or son, or a very difficult situation. Our cry, our plea, our prayers are for rescue or removal. Let's be honest. We normally look at life from a self-centered perspective. If the truth would be known, you've prayed for things to be taken out of your life that you've never admitted to anyone—your mama, your girlfriend, your pastor.

God is answering us the same way he answered Paul. He says, "My grace is sufficient for you. For my strength is made perfect in weakness." That is one of the ways of God. God's way produces divine strength through human weakness.

Do you want God's power? Strength comes to maturity in your life when you are weak. Unfortunately, we don't always get God's message. We are still centering our lives around ourselves. God's perspective is too foreign for us. When he refuses to answer our prayer to take us out of the situation or take away the problem, God is actually saying to us, "This is not about you. This is about my grace."

GRACE—GOD'S STRENGTH

We all need lots of grace, which is God's strength, to make it on a daily basis. When we submit ourselves to God, we get grace from God. The grace of God comes with humility, as James puts it:

But He gives more grace. Therefore He says:

> "God resists the proud,
> But gives grace to the humble."

Therefore submit to God. Resist the devil and he will flee from you. Draw near to God and He will draw near to you. Cleanse your hands, you sinners; and purify your hearts, you double-minded. Lament and mourn and weep! Let your laughter be turned to mourning and your joy to gloom. Humble yourselves in the sight of the Lord, and He will lift you up. (James 4:6-10)

What does the word *submit* mean? According to *Webster's Dictionary*, it means to yield oneself to the authority or will of another; to surrender; to defer to or consent to abide by the opinion or authority of another. To submit to God, we surrender our way of doing things. When we think we should behave one way, we defer to his way. We're used to being strong, but we surrender to weakness.

If African American women are to become vessels in God's hands that he desires to use, we will have to change our way of being strong to God's way of being weak. It's in submitting to God and doing things his way that we get close and stay close to God. Thinking like God and acting in his higher ways will transform our lives and allow us to become change agents.

The reason we want to be so strong is that we are not aware of the ways of God. I hate to make mistakes. I'm a perfectionist. Yet I want all God has for me. So I've prayed for God to do whatever it takes to have his way in my life. Well, since his way of divine strength is through human weakness, let me tell you what that has meant for me personally. It's meant making public mistakes. It's meant missing his timing in things he has called me to do. It's meant making mistakes that affected others and having to admit that I've missed it.

A Contradiction in Terms

If we are going to be keys to change, we all have to change our view of strength and weakness. God does not want to use the "strong black Christian woman." That's a contradiction in terms. When the strong black woman becomes a Christian, she has to learn to lean on God. She has to see strength from a different perspective. She has to learn to delight in weakness. God is going to use the woman who delights in her weakness but walks in the strength of the Lord and the power of his might. It's really about God.

We Didn't Do This With Our Own Might

God's hand has been on African American women for a long time. We have not always recognized his hand, but the ability to take a life of lemons and make lemonade is a God thing. Yes, let's recognize the accomplishments of great African American women. Let's acknowledge that many achieved greatness in spite of adversity. But let's give credit where credit is due. All great accomplishments come from God.

I am reminded of King Nebuchadnezzar, who looked around at all he had accomplished and began to take credit for it all. He said, "I, by my own mighty power, have built this beautiful city" (Daniel 4:30 NLT). As a result, God judged him. He was driven out of the palace to live with the animals in the field, eating grass with the cows. At the end of seven years, he looked up to heaven acknowledging and honoring God. God restored his sanity and his kingdom.

I fear that if black women continue to take the credit for keeping things together because of some inherent strength we possess, we could end up in the same condition as King Nebuchadnezzar. There have been many times when we didn't know what to do, when we have been weak and God came through. And we tend to take the credit for even that which God does. So instead of responding with nods and amens, we should be responding, "If it wasn't for the Lord, where would I be?" We should be saying, "It was the Lord's strength, not mine."

Since the phrase "strong black Christian woman" is a contradiction in terms, we're going to use SBW to refer to a "strong black woman" who does not know the Lord or an African American Christian woman who is either confused or still living in the strength of natural flesh, which is not in keeping with God's purposes. So if you are a strong black Christian woman who wants to change, get ready for weakness.

3

God Is Looking
for a Few Weak Women

If we desire to see more of God's strength in our families and our communities, we must be willing to be weak. We must be willing to delight in weakness.

Recently, I had to admit that I missed it. For about three years, we had conducted a leadership training institute for women who desire to minister to other women. I felt the Lord had called us to do this, but it became apparent that the help was not there to make it happen. We decided to suspend the institute until we had the help needed.

Well, this was difficult for me. I don't like to start things and then quit because I'm not able to accomplish them. It makes me feel like a failure. I also don't like disappointing others. Women had started the program with the goal to complete it. Now they would have to be told that their training would be put on hold.

Obviously I would love to have a relationship with God that would guarantee I would never make any mistakes. He could just communicate to me everything that he wanted and I would follow him flawlessly. I want you to see the point here. I want things to be this way so that I'll never look bad to others. That's not God's goal for my life. His goal is that I live my life in total dependence on him. In fact, he may purposely orchestrate things in my life that make me look bad.

I really want what God wants for me, but I can easily become confused. On one hand, I want to be strong in the Lord. On the other hand, I would like to be known as a strong black woman who is able to do everything all by myself. You know, superwoman—able to leap over tall buildings, dodge bullets and fly like a plane.

In other words, as a superwoman, I delight in the fact that I can take the children back and forth to school, music lessons and the church youth club. At the same time, I make sure there's food in the house and everyone has nutritious meals, and I attempt to keep the house clean. I also am available for counseling or prayer for anyone who needs it. I am committed to spending quality time with my husband, and I try to be available for friends. I do not neglect parent-teacher conferences, and when they need a parent to accompany my son's class to the zoo, guess who goes? Yet I still have deadlines for books and articles. I still have to manage a business *and* a ministry. There are bills to pay, invoices to send out, budgets to write and board meetings to plan, as well as meeting planners, bookkeepers, attorneys and others to deal with.

Yes, even I still try to be a strong black woman. I really think I can do everything; then I feel bad when it becomes obvious I can't and some things are slipping. I have a perfectionist tendency. In the natural, I don't like to admit I can't do it all. I don't like to admit I need help, and I don't like to ask for help. But I am growing in that area. It's definitely not as bad as it used to be.

However, I still have superwoman syndrome. I take on more than I can handle and at times I feel overwhelmed, like I'm sinking. Sometimes when my son asks, "What's for dinner?" I don't know and don't care, and I could very easily go off on him and anyone else close by. Could God be letting me feel overwhelmed as a means of getting my attention? Is it a way of teaching me to lean on his grace instead of my own self-sufficiency?

For me, being weak may mean I need to admit I can't do it all. It may mean asking others to step in and help. Being weak may mean having to say, "I don't know." It may mean not fully understanding things. It may mean not defending myself. It may mean having others wrongfully think badly of me. But it's not about me anyway.

DELIGHTING IN WEAKNESS

Oh, that we would get to the place of delighting in weakness. In 2 Corinthians, the apostle Paul said that he delighted in weakness. Weakness is not something most of us delight in. African American women often take the opposite view. We despise weakness. We hate weak people. Don't let a man who appears weak come into our lives. PLEEASE!

We surely do not want to appear to have any weakness ourselves. That would be unthinkable. Unfortunately this is true for Christian black women. We delight in being SBWs even though, for us, it is a contradiction of terms. Still, we relish that title. In most cases, we are referring to the strength that comes from our own inner fortitude, not the strength of the Lord.

It's in our weakness that God's strength is perfected and made mature in us. When we really understand the ways of God, we will say, like Paul, "Therefore most gladly I will rather boast in my infirmities, that the power of Christ may rest upon me" (2 Corinthians 12:9). When he finally understood that the only way he was going to have God's strength was through weakness, that was the beginning of Paul's understanding of the ways of God.

Paul knew he couldn't deal with that demon by himself. He needed God's strength. And since God had specifically told him, "My strength is at its best when you're weak, Paul," Paul's attitude was, "Fine, if that's the way it is, then let me be weak. I delight in weakness. I'd rather boast in my infirmities so that the power of Christ may rest on me. Therefore I take pleasure in infirmities, in reproaches, in persecutions, in distresses. Why? For Christ's sake. Why? For when I am weak, then I am strong."

Likewise, when we get the revelation and begin to understand the ways of God, we too will begin to delight in weakness. Then as we face the circumstances in our lives that are making us weak, we will understand that God's strength has the chance of being demonstrated in us.

It's not about me anymore. It never was about me, or you. It was always about God, God in me and in you. However, God only manifests himself in you as you decrease and he increases. And one of the ways you decrease is to have stuff that you can't handle, things going on that you don't like.

Personally, I have seen this over and over again in my speaking. The times God has shown up the most powerfully were the times I felt the weakest. It seemed like right before I would speak, something would come up, and I wouldn't have time to prepare like I wanted, or my emotions would be in disarray because of a misunderstanding with a friend or family member. I remember being told that my father had been diagnosed with prostate cancer just before I was leaving to speak. I didn't think I could do it. After a while, I just got used to God wanting me weak so that he would be my strength when I spoke to his chosen vessels.

ARE WE THERE YET?

Leaning doesn't come naturally; we have to learn how to do it. I am learning to be weak. I am learning to lean. I am learning to be comfortable in imperfection. Many of us don't know how to lean. I can't quite say that I'm there yet. I might not delight in weaknesses, reproaches or infirmities; however, I don't complain like I used to, and I desire to come to the place of delighting in them. I've asked God to make it true in me. That's what I want. I want the power of God to be evident in all I do. I want to live my life being strong in the Lord and in the power of his might.

God continues to allow me to encounter situations for which I feel totally incapable and unprepared. I'm recognizing these circumstances to be the answer to the prayer of strength perfected in weakness. Before, I would ask the Lord over and over to take a negative situation away from me. But now, after praying about it a few times, I hear him say, "My grace is sufficient for you. My strength is made perfect in weakness."

God and I don't have as many rifts because I'm beginning to see things from his point of view. Instead of looking at life from a self-centered perspective, I now see impossibilities as opportunities to die to my strength and allow his strength to come through.

It really is liberating. However, I still don't care for looking stupid when I have to say, "I don't know what I'm going to do." I still like to make a good impression on others. I'm just being honest. But I'm getting more comfortable with not knowing everything and not being in control.

THE PROCESS OF DECREASING

My friend Victoria has had a lot happen in her life that has been perplexing, difficult and painful (she is currently writing a book on pain). She has been mad at God because her life didn't turn out the way she had envisioned it. She married a preacher. And the way she had it figured out, they were going to raise their four children, have a nice, stable, happy family and work together in ministry for the duration of their married lives.

Her husband had two seminary degrees, and she had worked in ministry before they were married. It just seemed natural that they would minister together and live happily ever after. They had read all of the books about making marriage work. It had to work out.

But it didn't. After serving as a pastor in the church and preaching his head off, her husband was asked to leave. The church did not want a pastor that put that much emphasis on the Bible. Her husband was devastated. This was his life. He never quite recovered. He went from being a strong Christian to dabbling in questionable religious philosophies.

At this point in time they are separated. Victoria functions as a single parent and struggles with her husband's lack of interest in their children. God is simply not a part of his life in the way he used to be. He still talks about God, but it's apparent that God is not in control of how he lives his life. How can this be? It was not supposed to end up like this.

Vikki has also struggled with God over control of her life. She has battled depression, overeating, out-of-control anger and a host of other things. Though she hasn't abandoned God, she has been the SBW through it all. But God is slowly wearing down her strength. In its place, she has begun to change her perspective about how she thought it should be. Her focus is now off her husband and what he has done wrong. She is looking at the big picture of her opportunity to relate to many other women who have gone through similar trauma.

God has called her to minister to hurting women. If she knew she would have to go through all of the pain that she's been through, she may not have answered the call. But God has been faithful to her. He is showing her how much he wants to be her friend, her kinsman redeemer. She is experiencing the promise in Isaiah 54:5 of the Lord as her maker and her husband. God is looking out for her in tangible ways, and her life with God has reached a whole new level.

We must have trials and troubles in order to grow more dependent on God. That just doesn't make sense to us. It's not the way we think. It's not our way of handling things. We think God needs to come down to us. "God, can you come walk with me?" God answers with a gentle (and if necessary, not so gentle) voice: "No. You come and follow me. I'll show you where to walk."

OUR APPROACH IS TO GET RID OF WEAKNESS

I've asked God to help me get rid of my weaknesses. But why would he want to do that when his way is to delight in them? In 2 Corinthians chapter 4, we find more of Paul's philosophy about the hard things he encountered in life.

> But we have this treasure in earthen vessels, that the excellence of the power may be of God and not of us. We are hard pressed on every side, yet not crushed; we are perplexed, but not in despair; persecuted, but not forsaken; struck down, but not destroyed—always carrying about in the body the dying of the Lord Jesus, that the life of Jesus also may be manifested in our body. For we who live are always delivered to death for Jesus' sake, that the life of Jesus also may be manifested in our mortal flesh. So then death is working in us, but life in you. (2 Corinthians 4:7-12)

Paul knew what it meant to die to his flesh. In fact he talks about dying daily (1 Corinthians 15:31). It's when we die to self (what *we* want, what *we* feel and what *we* think) that the life of God is manifested through us. Christ is the treasure that lives in our earthen vessel. Christ needs to be seen. It is not about us, it's about Christ in us. As John the Baptist indicated in John 3:30, "He must increase but I must decrease." Death works in us during the hard times, but life works through us as a result.

THE TREASURE IN EARTHEN VESSELS

Again, Paul has come to a place of comprehending God's ways. All of the difficulties he talked about—being pressed on every side, perplexed, persecuted and struck down—were working death in him. The purpose was to get to the treasure. The treasure is there. It's just buried under too much self.

Times of weakness force us to dig beneath our strength to that which comes from the Lord. Unfortunately some of us are so strong in ourselves that it takes a lot to get to the treasure. When our strength is human strength, black women can be too strong for their own good and for the good of God to come forth. In our own strength, we don't rely on God. Because we have such well-developed soul strength, it takes mega-trouble for us to give up and rely on God's strength.

As Paul speaks to believers in Christ, he reiterates that all things are for their sakes, since they are in Christ, the center of the universe, and Christ is in them. Ultimately, the glory goes to God. Paul cites the purpose of all things:

> For all things are for your sakes, that grace, having spread through the many, may cause thanksgiving to abound to the glory of God.
>
> Therefore we do not lose heart. Even though our outward man is perishing, yet the inward man is being renewed day by day. For our light affliction, which is but for a moment, is working for us a far more exceeding and eternal weight of glory, while we do not look at the things which are seen, but at the things which are not seen. For the things which are seen are temporary, but the things which are not seen are eternal. (2 Corinthians 4:15-18)

As Paul continues his discourse, we see that he is concerned for God's glory. Paul does not have to lose heart because his outward man is perishing; his inward man (the treasure) is being renewed day by day. That's why he can call all he went through "light afflictions."

How can afflictions be light? Afflictions are the troubles we have in life. They are a burden. They are heavy. How can Paul call them light? He can call them light because he had God's perspective on his trials. Jesus also called his burden light (Matthew 11:30). Paul saw his difficulties as lasting only for a season—"but for a moment." I guess he knew troubles don't last always. We need to face our difficulties with the truth that "this too shall pass." This is just momentary. I can hang in here and walk through this. And as I go through, I will come out better. God's grace will be a greater part of my life.

Paul also had the God-given perspective that his afflictions were working something much more important in his life—an eternal weight of glory. He describes this weight of glory as far more exceeding. That means it surpassed the light affliction in importance. He also describes it as being eternal rather than temporal. The glory that the light affliction was going to accomplish in his life was going to last forever. That's a long time compared to perhaps a couple of years or even seventy years of going through stuff down here.

Most of us want it down here *and* up there. That's fine. I believe we have enough indication in the Word of God that he truly delights in blessing his children down here. I'm just saying there's a time for everything. There is a time to bask in his blessings. There is also a time to volunteer for war. At that time a good soldier has to give up his rights to some of the things that were normal before. A good soldier does not entangle himself with the affairs of this life (2 Timothy 2:4).

God is calling African American women to volunteer in an army that will manifest the defeat of Satan that was accomplished on the cross. Those who are willing need to prepare mentally and spiritually for battle—not in our strength as SBWs but in the strength found when leaning on him.

The times we live in require a different level of sobriety. Peter talks about a time in which we need to live our lives differently (2 Peter 4:7). I believe we are in a time when African American women will have to purposely go to another level of strength. Let us follow Paul as he followed Christ. Let us also delight in weaknesses. Let us look at our difficulties as light afflictions. Let us be concerned about digging down to the treasure that dwells in our earthen vessels. Chosen vessels are meant to display the treasure of God, letting God get the credit.

SBW, it's not about our strength anymore. Maybe we have been able to handle more than most humans have handled, but what's coming in the future will be different. A man accused of killing his wife and unborn child, a man shooting his four children and then setting his house on fire, a blackout affecting over fifty million people. Are those signs of the times? Only God can handle the demonic onslaught that has been targeted against our minds, our families and our communities.

God is looking for a few weak women. Will you be a weak woman who walks in God's strength because you have learned to delight in weakness?

4

Letting God Be God

The goal of the Christian walk is to let Christ in us be the reflection of our life. We die to self and allow Christ's life to take us over. Although Christ's life is in us, much of the time we do not allow his life to be manifested. We need to decrease and the life of Christ needs to increase in its visible expression.

The Scriptures tell us that we are in Christ. They also tell us that Christ is in us. When we receive Christ, he puts his Spirit within us. Note the italicized words in these passages:

> Set your mind on things above, not on things on the earth. For you died, and *your life is hidden with Christ in God.* (Colossians 3:2-3, emphasis mine)

> I have been crucified with Christ; it is no longer I who live, but *Christ lives in me;* and the life which I now live in the flesh I live by the faith of the Son of God, who loved me and gave Himself for me. (Galatians 2:20, emphasis mine)

> His divine power has given to us all things that pertain to life and godliness. (2 Peter 1:3)

Who's in Control?

We mentioned in the first chapter that African American women may have to make some changes. One change is to give up the need for control. Strong black women like to be in control. We like to know what's going on with everyone in our lives. "Where you been?" "Where you going?" We convince ourselves that we have to be in everybody's business—of course, it's all for their good. To consider that maybe we need to entrust some of our loved ones into God's care even when we don't know all the details of their lives is a strange consideration. We wouldn't even think of it. It's our right to know. After all, we're SBWs.

But God wants control; he is not there just in case we're in trouble. God didn't send his Son Jesus to help us; Jesus came to live in us and through us. There is a difference between someone helping you live your life and someone living the life for you.

Most Christians have the wrong perspective when it comes to God's life. "Lord, I have this heavy load to lift. Could you just get on the other side over there and help me with this load?" That's how we treat God concerning all of the things in our lives, whether it is forgiving another, studying the Word, praying or sharing our faith. We want to do it with his help.

God is saying, "No, it isn't about you calling on me when you need help. I want my life in you to be your life. You don't have to call for me to come help you. Just realize I'm there all the time. You don't have to shout to tell me to come. You just have to quietly begin talking. I'm already there waiting to listen."

God wants us out of the way so that he can do it by his power in our earthen vessels. But we don't want to give up control. In fact, particularly as women, we have a problem with control—sometimes big problems with control! We need and want God, but we aren't giving up control.

THE PROCESS OF SPIRITUAL GROWTH

The level of control that Christ displays in our life depends on our level of maturity. There are four stages of Christian growth: baby, child, youth and adult. Although he is in our life throughout each stage, Christ is not in complete control until we become adults. In the first three stages, Christ is in our life, but we have yet to grow in grace and in the knowledge of Christ in us. In each stage, we make choices. The more choices we make that are in accordance with the ways of God as recorded in his Word, the quicker we grow. But we can have Christ in our life and still live by the memory of our old life source.

Jesus used a lot of parables to depict life in the kingdom. In these parables, he uses natural things that the people of that day could identify with to describe the things that could not be seen, the things of the spiritual kingdom.

In this chapter, I will be using a couple of picture stories to illustrate the process of spiritual growth. Please don't get caught up with the details. There will not be a perfect theological fit. These are just pictures to help us see the process of spiritual growth. The point of this book is to help us understand that it is not about us. God is interested in our spiritual maturity even more than our developing complete understanding.

THE CAR ANALOGY

Before we become Christians, it's as if we are driving our own car, but we keep running off the side of the road and ending up in the ditch. A nice man always shows up and helps us put the car back on the road. After he helps us, he seems to stand there with a longing in his eye. We get back in the car, thank him, wave and go on our way. Then we end up in the ditch again.

After a while, because we have so many mishaps and this kind gentleman is always there to help us, we decide that maybe it would be good to have him in our car (life). We find out his name is Jesus Christ and we invite him in. He accepts our invitation and stands for a minute, waiting to see what side we get in on. We hop in the driver's seat, and he opens the passenger side and takes a seat. While getting in, he tells us that he knows how to drive. We say, "Oh no, I don't need you to drive. I would just like to have you around for when I go into the ditch. I can drive okay." He says, "When I get in a car, I get in to drive. I will eventually have to drive, but I will not force you out of the driver's seat now." You look at him a little strangely but start the car up and drive away.

You are a Christian now, a baby Christian. But Christ is in your life, and you're on your way through the journey of life. However, you keep running into the ditch. It almost seems it happens more now than before. Each time Christ gets out and puts the car back on the road, he stands waiting to see what side you get in on. You always get in on the driver's side, ignoring his offer to drive. As time goes on, you grow a little. As you talk to your new rider, you find he is safe. You are getting a little tired. So after running into the ditch many times, you finally accept his offer to drive. You get in on the passenger's side.

Now you are a child Christian. Christ is in your life and he is driving. You're on the passenger's side, but although you were initially sleepy, you're now wide awake. In fact, you're trying to help him drive. You see a curve and you're not sure if he sees it, so you grab the wheel and try to turn into the curve. Well, since you're steering from the passenger's side, you run into the ditch again. The car hadn't gone in the ditch all the time Christ was driving, but when you tried to help, it happens again.

Well, that happens over and over. You try to brake. You try to steer the car. You get in the way. It's time for another growth phase. The next time you interfere with his driving and run into the ditch, when you're ready to get back on the road, he opens the back door and suggests you get in. You really are sleepy and this would allow you to stretch out, so you don't protest. You get in.

Now you're in the back seat. You are now a youth. Not a child, yet not an adult. You nod a little, but you're still not sure if you can trust the driver. There are some places you want to go. You'd better keep one eye open. As you continue down the road of life, you yell at him for not taking the exit you wanted. You pout over the exits he does take. You tell him to speed up. He is going entirely too slow, not one bit over the limit. Sometimes you just want to take it easy, and you yell at him for going too fast. The car is full of tension. You can't reach the brake and steering wheel from the back seat, but you sure are trying to tell him how to drive your car.

It's time for another growth phase. So Christ stops the car, pulls over on the side of the road and waits. At first, you don't say anything. Maybe he's taking a nap. But the wait goes on for hours and then days. You begin to get impatient. "Wait a minute, what's going on here?" you ask.

"I'm just waiting," he says. Another hour passes.

"Why are we waiting?" you ask.

"I'm waiting for you to go to sleep," he informs you.

Defiantly, you determine, *Well, he's going to wait forever because I'm not going to just go to sleep and let him take me wherever he wants to without my input.*

That seems okay with him. He acts like he has all the time in the world.

Finally, you do enter the last stage—you fall asleep in the back seat. He waits until he's sure you're in a deep sleep and pulls back onto the road. He's now free to do what needs to be done and you go on to your destiny. He's driving. Your spirit, empowered by his spirit, now has freedom to do what is needed in your life, while your mind, will and emotions are asleep.

While sleeping, you are not passive. Your tendency to want to know everything, control things and operate out of your own personal desires is put to sleep (death), but your spirit is fully awake (Isaiah 51:9; Romans 13:11). In this state, your mind, will and emotions are now tools of the Spirit, rather than the life force of your existence. Essentially you have died and the life of Christ is now your life. You are fully alive because your mind, will and emotions are under the control of the Holy Spirit.

THE HOUSE ANALOGY

Let's look at another picture that describes what goes on when we accept Christ. This time I'm going to use a picture of a house. Using the analogy of a house to depict our Christian walk is not new. There is a popular book called *My Heart—Christ's Home* that does that.

Your body is like a house. Your spirit is the occupant, and your personality is like the furniture inside your house. In the house, the furniture may be a telephone, a refrigerator, a computer, a bed, a sofa, a closet, a table and some other items. So the furniture (the personality) and the occupant (the spirit) are in the house (a body). In other words, your body is the home to your personality and your human spirit.

Before you are born again, everything in this house is dead. The basic definition of death is separation. We speak of death here to mean that everything is separated from the life of God. Before we become children of God through Jesus Christ, we are children of Satan. Satan is the Lord of the house, and the prevailing atmosphere of the home is death and self-centeredness.

When you become a Christian, God comes into your house and kills and buries the person that was there, then comes in the person of Jesus and takes residence in your house. Jesus is now the life source of your new house. The old life force (death and self-centeredness) that came from Satan is gone.

Now you are a new creation. God—through his Son Jesus Christ and the Holy Spirit—is the new occupant in your house. His life is the prevailing ambiance of your home. Your mind, will and emotions are still there as furniture, the personality of the house. Your body did not change. But instead of darkness coming through the windows, there is plenty of light.

This house with the new occupant is entirely new. The new occupant will now want to use your personality (what you think, feel and want—the furniture) to reflect how he operates. You have an entirely new occupant in the house who will do things totally different than the old owner.

Unfortunately, some of us invite Christ into our house as owner and resident, but we treat him like a guest instead. We say, "Okay, come in. Have a seat."

"I didn't come to sit down," he says. "I came in to take over. I came in to rearrange everything. I want to go into that closet over there."

"Oh no! No, no, no, no! Nobody goes in that closet. No; sorry."

"Well, can I go into the kitchen?"

"I have a nice sofa for you right here. Could you just sit down?"

"But I would like to go into the bedroom."

"You better stay out of that bedroom! Sit here on this sofa. I invited you in my house as my guest, so would you please sit down."

"But look, I have some supplies. I want to do some cleaning in here."

"Look, I've been ruling this house ever since I've been here. I may need some help every now and then, so would you sit down? When I need a little help, I'll ask you. But in the meantime, just have a seat."

That was not in the bargain. When you gave your life to Christ, you were at a point where you said, "Come and take over; take everything, Lord!" You were so beat up by sin and Satan that you said, "Oh God, I need you!" He came in and said, "All right, let's do it. Let's get this thing done." And now you say, "No, sit down."

The new occupant has new plans for the telephone. He has plans for prayer and encouragement instead of gossip and slander. He has new plans for the thought patterns of the computer. He has brought in totally new computer programs that he wants to download.

When you signed the dotted line you said, "I give my everything to you. I will allow you to rule my mind, my will and my emotions. I release control over everything." That was the agreement.

But once he comes in, you say, "Well I didn't really mean it that way. I still want to have some control here myself. I just wanted to have help available when I need it. I wasn't really planning on letting you do it all. Just wait there in that corner over there, and I'll call you when I need you."

Now there's a fight over how the telephone is used. There's a fight over what gets programmed into the computer. You no longer want the new occupant to be in complete control.

THE REAL STRUGGLE

The struggle is flesh against the Spirit: the furniture trying to rule the house. The telephone remembers what used to go on over the telephone. So when the new owner says, "We're going to use the telephone to pray and bless people," the telephone says, "No, that isn't how it used to be. We gossiped. That's what I'm used to. I don't want any praising going on through me. I can't relate to that."

The new owner says, "But I bought this house. I now own everything here. I thought I could do what I wanted to here."

"No," the telephone says. "I'm not used to that. If you want to gossip and slander someone, I can help you there. I'm very familiar with that."

"That's what the old owner did. I'm the new owner. We'll do it my way."

"Well, that's just not me."

The table still knows what used to go on the table. The refrigerator remembers what used to be inside it. The bed remembers what used to go on in the bed. And the bed, table and refrigerator all say, "No that's not the way it used to be; we're going to keep it like it was. We don't like change. We're going to do it the way we used to do it."

What we have is the furniture ruling the house. The mind, will and emotions are ruling the house. Why? They're used to the old owner's way of ruling. They didn't know they would be servants to the new owner. They were used to being in control. That's the way the old owner let things happen.

If it feels good, do it. If it makes sense, then why not do it? That's the way your house was ruled under the old owner. The old owner supported your self-centered perspective. You could live it up. You could do what you wanted as long as you felt like it, or it made sense to you, or it was something you wanted to do. That's how your house was run. Never mind that you were going to an early grave because there was no discipline in what you ate, with whom you slept or how you treated others; you did have control. At least you thought you did.

Now the Holy Spirit says, "I am in control here. You relinquished your rights to think the way you want to think, to feel the way you've been used to feeling and to act the way you have always acted. You have relinquished that to me. Let's move on up and grow on up. I will now put my thoughts and my way of doing things in you."

But it is too painful. It hurts. And so we don't grow up because it hurts too much. It kills us. Because the Holy Spirit is not pushy and because God has given us free will, God will let us stay in our confused, carnal state of Christianity. But I warn you that if you really want God to be everything, even when you fight with him, God is determined to get us to the place where we realize it is not about us.

Are you ready to move on up? Yes, there will be pain in growing up; there are a lot of growing pains. But, if you refuse to grow up, you're still going to be in pain. You're hurting now anyway. You might as well hurt with some grace. The comfort of the Holy Spirit will heal the hurts. You don't have to live a lonely life, calling on God only when you need help. God wants to be an intimate part of your life every day.

5

TURN IN YOUR RESIGNATION

There can only be one God. If we want to be God, God will sit back and let us run our universe. The other alternative is to let God be God. Most of our problems with God have to do with our desire to understand. If we're no longer God, we do not need to understand. Yes, it would be nice to understand, but God has already told us to lean not on our own understanding. Instead, we are to acknowledge him and he will direct our paths (Proverbs 3:5-6). God did not intend for us to understand everything.

Come on now, how many times have you tried to counsel God on what is really needed for your life? Now, I know you might not want to admit it, but you've been trying to be a co-god. That's the whole motive of trying to control everything in your life. God does not need co-gods. God does not need our help in running the universe, not even in running our lives.

So all of us SBWs need to just turn it in. We need to turn in our resignation, stop trying to be in control and begin to rest in God's will and purposes, even when we don't understand what God is doing. We all just need to resign from the position of co-god. I suggest we write a letter of resignation. It could go something like this:

Dear God,

It's with much regret that I must inform you that I have decided to resign from my current position of co-god. It appears I do not have the needed qualifications.

As I was contemplating making this move, I knew you would want to know what prompted my decision. Though I hate to admit it, it just does not seem you need my help. I always get in the way and mess things up. I can think of several times in the last few weeks when I tried to do things the best way I knew how and it just did not work out.

Over and over, I get embarrassed because you always come up with a plan while I'm still in the process of trying to figure things out. Most of the times, provisions have just appeared out of nowhere. These are things I guess you knew about and kept behind the scene. You did not even bother to tell me. I guess you forgot. But frankly I'm a little tired of being left out. Imagine how stupid I felt when I was busy making preparations and you already had provisions that were unseen. You act like you don't need my help.

I find it is very difficult working with you. You and I just don't think alike. You are always so full of surprises. We have different ways of doing things. It's not that I don't appreciate all you do, but the way you do things makes me look like I don't know what I'm doing. I don't like that feeling. It really would be helpful if you discussed things with me. I get tired of you always telling me, "Just trust and obey," or "I've got it covered." What did you hire me for if you won't allow me to do any work?

What really ticked me off is that memo you sent around last week. You know, the one that read, "This is God. I'll be taking care of all of your problems today." My name was not even on the memo as co-god. It has become very apparent to me that you don't even recognize my position. I should have seen it coming. You never consult with me or ask for my opinion about anything.

It's just too hard having this job in name only, so I'm quitting. I apologize for such a short notice, but my resignation is effective immediately. I can't take this job anymore! I think you work much better alone. So you can just be God all by yourself!

While I'm at it, I want to get a few other things off my chest. You act like you are so big. I mean you walk around acting like you own everything. And that whole thing about you being the only one that can determine good and evil . . . that really bugs me. There were many things I thought were bad but you said were good. I expressed my opinions to everyone, too; but like always, you come up smelling like roses with your uncanny way of making the bad good. Everybody is always talking about how good you are. I get so sick of everyone singing your praises. If only given a chance, I could show everyone that I am as capable as you are.

Anyway, my mind is made up. This is my final decision. Don't even try to talk me out of it. I wouldn't come back, even if you got down on your hands and knees and begged me.

Sincerely yours,

*P.S. God, it was you that hired me, wasn't it? I must have misplaced the letter
in which you first offered the job to me. I can't find it anywhere.*

I hope you are laughing after reading that letter. Can you believe
someone would actually say those things to *God?* It sounds so presump-
tuous and rather stupid. But think about it, isn't that how we sometimes
act? We really think we know how to run things better than God. That's
the real reason why we don't do the things he tells us to do. That's why
we're always giving him our advice. We think we know better than
God.

I've turned in my letter of resignation. Actually, I've turned it in a
few times. I may have to turn it in again if I try to go back to work. I
sure hope I won't be that dense. And you cannot imagine how hard it
is trying to hold up the whole universe on these human shoulders. Let
me tell you that it really is a load off. Perhaps you need to let it go as
well.

It is really stressful trying to be everywhere at all times, seeing what everybody is doing. Just thinking about how I tried to be co-god is tiring. I
trust you will give it up too. In fact, feel free to use the above letter (even
though you might want to reword it with less attitude). God is just not going to share the position of co-god with anyone. He's God all by himself.

WHO TOLD YOU THAT YOU WERE MS. FIX-IT?

A few weeks ago, I was blessed by something shared by someone I have
known for a number of years. A situation happened in her family, and
she made a decision that came back to haunt her. She describes herself
as a seventy-year-old granny and great-granny. She had a degree and career in early childhood development and education. She prided herself
in being "the greatest grandmother that a kid could ever want or need."
She loved her grandchildren and they loved her.

A few of Louise's (not her real name) grandchildren and great-grand-
children were over at her house one day when one of the teens and one
of the younger ones were alone in the basement. The two denied any
inappropriate behavior. She gave them a warning and decided to mon-
itor everyone a little more carefully. But she made the decision not to
mention this to the adult members of her family.

About a year and a half later, the little one involved in the incident admitted she did not want to come to Louise's house and told why. After the allegations were made known, both the mother of the teen and the mother of the little one were upset. They were not speaking to each other. The little child's mother was really having a hard time dealing with the situation. She wanted to physically hurt the teen, and she did not want to see or talk to Louise.

Louise was distraught. She knew that this situation could tear her family apart. She tried to fix everything. The very thing she prided her-self in—being a granny everyone loved and a woman who knew how to take care of children—was crumbling.

Louise and her daughter, the grandmother of the little one, cried, prayed and depended on the Lord for help and understanding. About six to eight months later, as she cried out to the Lord, Louise asked him why he let this happen to her.

In Louise's own words, "Finally the Lord answered me very loudly and clearly and asked me, 'Who told you that you were Ms. Fix-It?' At first I didn't know why the Lord was talking to me this way. I wanted him to feel sorry for me and give me comfort and deliver us from all this hurt and unforgiveness. After continuing to pray, he asked me again, 'Who told you that you were Ms. Fix-It?'

"When I realized who was talking to me, I was amazed. I fell on my knees and said, 'I hear you, Lord. I repent of my sin of exalting myself. I repent for leaning on my own understanding. I pray that you will speak to my loved ones and ease their pain as you're doing for me.'"

Louise testifies that the Lord has done a lot of mending for everyone involved. She thinks that they could never have been healed if it wasn't for God. They have even been brought closer together, and Louise is ex-tremely grateful to the Lord. She says, "In my daily walk, when I hear that parents, grandparents and great-grandparents are experiencing dif-ficulty in helping their loved ones, I ask them the same question the Lord asked me, 'Who told you that you are Ms. Fix-It?'"

IT'S DIFFERENT WITH GOD IN CONTROL

Let me tell you a little of what it will be like after you turn in your res-ignation. Life is going to be a little different. You have always had everything under control. You've always been so self-confident. As a result of God taking over and controlling your life, you will face things you cannot fix. Now you have no confidence in anything or anybody, much less in yourself. You depend on God now. You pray all the time. When people say, "What are you going to do?" you say, "I don't know."

Ten years ago you would have never said, "I don't know." You would have a program and a plan, and you would be executing it before the ink dried on the paper. That's how efficient you were. Now some years later, after God has taken you through a whole lot, you don't know what to do. What happened?

Because you turned in your resignation, you gave God permission to show up. God came in the midst of your circumstances to truly be God, and he began to show you himself. He made it clear you can't do this. He answered you and said, "No, you need me."

You used to pray before you went to bed, now you pray all the time. You used to pray when you went to church and when you got up in the morning, but now you pray all day long. You're praying, "God help me." "Lord, you better guide this car for me." "Lord, help me not go off on her." "Lord, I need your strength to make it through this meeting." "Lord, help."

Other people see the things God is doing behind the scene. Your friends at church or work see that you're more patient now. Your girl-friends see that you're less apt to walk in pride. They see a new humility. Why? The very trial that you thought was so terrible has humbled you.

You may not see any change. In fact, you might feel like you're a basket case. You feel dumb, weak, out of sorts. The self-confidence is gone. Yes, the switch is being made. Your confidence is switching over to the Lord. You have been changed in the process of going through. God has worked some things into you and has worked some things out of you. He has worked out pride, impatience, giving up too quickly, independence and overconfidence. In its place, he has instilled humility, patience, perseverance, interdependence and dependence on God.

My Personal Flesh Struggles

Don't think the change God does in us comes overnight. Sometimes it will take years. Many of us are so entrenched in our old patterns that it takes a while before we submit to the change God is trying to do in us. Many times it takes a long time because change can be painful.

When my husband does or says something that I don't care for, I'll review the unfairness over and over in my head. Whenever I do that, I'll get even more upset. Eventually I don't want to be around him, so I'll withdraw emotionally. Then it becomes hard to be pleasant.

I used to think because I didn't get all up in his face, curse him out, and say cutting and biting things that I was demonstrating good Christian behavior. I wasn't deliberately hurting him. But I was still being an instrument of pain. In fact, the Lord showed me how I could be very cruel just by withdrawing. I did not consciously think, *I'm going to hurt my husband by withdrawing.* I just went into myself when I was in pain. In my mind, it was about me.

I don't do confrontation or speaking the truth in love well. I don't like conflict. I love peace. I'd rather hide my feelings if I think it's going to cause conflict or turmoil. But hiding feelings creates conflict within. God desires truth in the inner man. God has shown me that when I hide my feelings from myself and others I am living a lie. Truth sets us free. I have to face the truth of my emotions before I can experience healing. But it has been painful to change. It's much more comfortable to do things the old way.

Obviously, my old way may not be your old way. Each of us has old ways that are not godly. They are the ways of the flesh. All flesh is flesh. My flesh happens to be religious flesh. Unfortunately, that's the most dangerous kind of flesh. It is so deceiving.

I was doing what I thought was the Christian thing, being quiet, trying to please. I thought I was being forgiving. I found out later that I had big resentment and anger issues. I wasn't facing my true feelings. Deception keeps us in bondage.

That's where God has been changing me. God has allowed painful situations in my life to force me to confront the things inside of me. Going to God with my pain has been hard. It's not the way I'm used to doing things. I admit that when I'm hurt or when I'm confused about what is going on in my life, I often turn to food for comfort. But God is asking me to go to the people in my life and express my feelings to them. How can I do that when I've been hiding my feelings from myself?

I'm finding out that before I get to the place of expressing my thoughts and emotions to my husband, God wants me to express my pain to him. I've been slowly learning to stop mulling things over in my mind and just tell the Lord what I'm feeling. He helps me sort out the emotions. He gives me comfort. Then when it is time to speak to my husband or someone else, I'm in a whole different frame of mind. Sometimes, just the feeling that I'm understood after having my talk with Jesus is all I need to make me okay.

We talk to ourselves and get more messed up; or we talk to our girlfriends or anyone else who will listen. The missing key is: we don't take our thoughts to God and allow him to sort them out by his Word.

God is asking us to cease from our labor and enter into his rest (Hebrews 4:11). He is not looking for us to be co-gods. He is looking for partners who will obey him and respond to his instructions. God is asking us to make major changes in our orientation about life. He wants us to know his perspective, his desire and his identity.

Part two

IT'S ALWAYS
BEEN ABOUT GOD

6

God's Perspective

Bᵤt Mom, I had planned to work this summer. I won't be able to go with you and Alex on that trip. It's just not the right time. Besides, I wanted to go to basketball camp too. I'm sorry but what I have planned for the summer will not work if I go on the family vacation."

"Listen, David, I have planned this vacation as something for us as a whole family. Remember what your Dad and I used to tell you when you were young? 'The world does not revolve around you!'"

If you are a public school teacher, a parent or anyone who is around young children, you may be familiar with their tendency to think as if the world centers on them. Although the above conversation is made up, Diane Proctor Reeder, a friend of mine, told me that when her two children were younger, she and her husband often had to remind them that they were not the center of the world. From a child's limited experience and perspective, it would be easy to come to that false conclusion.

By the time we get into our teens, most of us have had enough experiences that prove there is much more to life than our little world. By the time we become adults, we should have learned that it is important to accommodate and coordinate our lives with other people.

Recently, our family planned to drive to our niece, Mya's, college graduation. My oldest son, who is now living on his own, had planned to go with us but decided to do something else that same weekend. Well, since he is now a young adult, he did not ask us to adjust our plans to fit his plans. He purchased a plane ticket to fly in after his plans were over. A few years ago, he probably would have wanted us to adjust our plans to accommodate him, but he didn't even ask. He's growing up. Adults realize they have to do the adjustment; children want everyone else to adjust to them.

CHILDISH THINKING

I think few adults would consciously admit to having the delusion that the world revolves around them. Normally, they have learned to adjust their lives to others. However, there is probably a significant number of adults who are still totally selfish, who really haven't grown up.

Though we may have learned to make adjustments in our thinking as we relate to people, perhaps we have not made the same adjustment in our thinking as we relate to God. Sometimes our response to the situations we encounter indicates some aspect of the childish thinking that the spiritual world revolves around us.

We rarely consider events in life from God's perspective. We all need to appreciate that there is one center of the universe. Our relationship to that center is what it is all about. It's not about us. The true center of the universe wants us to see things from his perspective.

There are facts we see on the surface; and there is a set of factors that is beneath the surface, beyond what we see with our physical eyes. The true center of the universe is not seen with physical eyes. When all of the facts are in and when all of the factors are factored in, it may surprise us to discover that although we have focused only on the visible realities usually related to ourselves, it really is not about us.

Many of the challenges in our lives are intended to get us to live on a higher spiritual plane than we are accustomed to. Our new identity in Christ is very real, but it often takes a back seat to what we can see and our usual pattern of operating and thinking. God's task is to get us to live out of our new identity in Christ and turn away from the way we have been used to acting and reacting.

GROWING IN GRACE AND KNOWLEDGE

Jesus is the sum of all spiritual things. Jesus is the sum of all things. Everything is about God. God has made his Son Jesus the beneficiary of all he has. Jesus is the beginning, the end, the Alpha and the Omega. Jesus is in God and God is in Jesus (John 17:21). As a Christian, you are in Jesus and Jesus is in you (Colossians 3:3, 11; Ephesians 2:13). Jesus, the center of the universe, is all you need.

You already have all you need. Jesus has given you all you need to live this life in a godly fashion (2 Peter 1:3). Everything that happens in your life is to give you a greater understanding of what you already have in Christ. When you have a situation that shows a lack—whether it's a lack of wisdom, finances or strength—God desires for you to grow in his strength (grace) and to have a greater revelation of Jesus in you (knowledge). Our entire Christian walk is to bring us growth in grace and in the knowledge of Jesus Christ. Jesus is all we need. We need to know all of who Jesus is.

To come to a greater knowledge of God's strength, we have to learn to depend less on our strength—our ability to fix it. The crises in our lives are designed to force us to lean on Jesus, the help we already have within. But in the meantime, we will be disappointed with those we had depended on in the past for help. God will cut off help from every place so that you only have him.

Jesus is the center of our lives, whether we acknowledge it or not. But that doesn't mean we're not important. God has designed each event in our lives especially for us, to reveal the many facets of his greatness. When God allows a great host of enemies to come against you, it is to reveal how much bigger he is than your enemies. The greater your problem, the more God desires to show you his greatness.

We would have the peace and rest of God if we looked at life's problems from the perspective of getting to know God better.

IT'S ALL ABOUT HIM!

What would your life look like if it was centered around God? Would that change how you behave on your job? Would it change how you relate to your parents? Would it change how you relate to your family members? Many of us give God his due on Sunday mornings, but the rest of the week is spent centered around me, myself and I. God deserves much more than that.

Jesus has supremacy in all things. All things have been created by him and for him. This is made clear in the following passage of Scripture found in Colossians 1:

Thanks to the Father who has qualified us to be partakers of the inheritance of the saints in the light. He has delivered us from the power of darkness and conveyed us into the kingdom of the Son of His love, in whom we have redemption through His blood, the forgiveness of sins. He is the image of the invisible God, the firstborn over all creation. For by Him all things were created that are in heaven and that are on earth, visible and invisible, whether thrones or dominions or principalities or powers. All things were created through Him and for Him. And He is before all things, and in Him all things consist. And He is the head of the body, the church, who is the beginning, the firstborn from the dead, that in all things He may have the preeminence. (Colossians 1:12-18)

In the book of Hebrews, we find more evidence that Jesus is the center of it all:

God, who at various times and in various ways spoke in time past to the fathers by the prophets, has in these last days spoken to us by His Son, whom He has appointed heir of all things, through whom also He made the worlds. (Hebrews 1:1-2)

As you continue to read the first chapter of the book of Hebrews, you'll find that the Son, Jesus, is compared to angels and declared better than angels:

For to which of the angels did He ever say:
  "You are My Son,
  Today I have begotten You"?
And again:
  "I will be to Him a Father,
  And He shall be to Me a Son"? . . .
But to the Son He says:
  "Your throne, O God, is forever and ever;
  A scepter of righteousness is the scepter of Your Kingdom.
  You have loved righteousness and hated lawlessness;
  Therefore God, Your God, has anointed You
  With the oil of gladness more than Your companions." . . .
  "They will perish, but You remain;

> And they will all grow old like a garment;
> Like a cloak You will fold them up,
> And they will be changed.
> But You are the same,
> And Your years will not fail." (Hebrews 1:5-6, 8-9, 11-12)

Hebrews also states:

> But we see Jesus, who was made a little lower than the angels, for
> the suffering of death crowned with glory and honor, that He, by
> the grace of God, might taste death for everyone.
>
> For it was fitting for Him, for whom are all things and by whom
> are all things, in bringing many sons to glory, to make the captain
> of their salvation perfect through sufferings. (Hebrews 2:9-10)

God, the center of the universe has made all things to center around
his Son, Jesus. All things are by him and all things are for him. Whatever exists in this world is for Jesus. Whatever happens in my life is for
Jesus. All things are for Jesus. Jesus, the Son of God, is who it is all
about. It's not about you.

If something you consider good happens in your life, it's not about
you. It's for Jesus. If something you consider bad happens in your life,
guess what? It's not about you; it's for Jesus. Everything is for Jesus. When
you go to worship with other saints, it's not to make you feel better; it's
for Jesus. If you happen to feel better as a result, that might be because
you are connected to Jesus. You get the benefits, but he gets the glory.

You go to work for Jesus. You get married for Jesus. You remain single
for Jesus. You have children for Jesus. You don't have children for Jesus.
You have the ability to get wealth for Jesus. You sell all you have and give
to the poor for Jesus. If you have given your all to Jesus, then your life is
for Jesus. Begin to see all of life for Jesus. The difficulty on your job is
for Jesus. The problems in your marriage are for Jesus. Your great relationship with your husband is for Jesus. The troubles you have with your
children are for Jesus. Your wonderful friendships are for Jesus. Your in-
law problems, boyfriend struggles, ex issues are all for Jesus. At least it
all can be, if you begin to relate to the center of the universe as the center of your life and cease thinking it is all about you.

GOD WANTS US TO IDENTIFY WITH HIM

God wants a people who identify with him and his agenda. He is seeking women who will be close to him. He is looking for African Americans to be close to him. In fact, he wants to be closer to African American women more than we want to be close to him.

Seeing things from God's perspective requires that we change our way of thinking. It requires that we change our way of responding to the events that go on in our life. To see things from God's perspective means we have to walk in agreement with him. When we understand life's challenges and circumstances from his perspective, we become close to God.

When we think it's about us, we think of our comfort as the critical goal in life. When we are self-focused, our desire to understand everything about what happens to us becomes important. When life centers on us, perfecting our ability to control things is one of our chief aims in life. When we approach life from a selfish perspective, we will inevitably move away from God rather than coming close.

We can be set free from the prison of our self-centered thinking. We can know truth, Jesus, and knowing truth will set us free (John 8:32). Jesus is the way, the truth and the life. No one comes to the Father except through Jesus (John 14:6). It is possible for us to change our thinking. That's the journey God wants to take us on. He wants us to grow in freedom. Jesus, God's Son, will set us free, and whom the Son sets free is free indeed (John 8:36).

Some of us have experienced freedom in Christ, but we have gone back into bondage. We need to stand in the liberty by which we have been made free and refuse to get entangled back under a yoke of bondage (Galatians 5:1). Many of us are confused and frustrated about the events in our life simply because we have not yet learned that there is something much more important than our individual comfort and our ability to understand or control the things that go on around us.

The world does not revolve around us. This is a good point for all to remember and consider over and over, but especially for those who believe in God. The world revolves around Jesus Christ, the Son of God (Colossians 1:12-18). When facing the events of life, the question we should begin to ask is, What about Jesus?

God has not only made his Son Jesus the center of the universe, he has made him the only means whereby we can have a relationship with God. Each of us has the opportunity to choose to be in Jesus by confessing with our mouth and believing in our heart that God raised Jesus from the dead (Romans 10:9). Our acceptance of Jesus' payment for our sins and his opening of the way to a relationship with God will place us in Jesus. Our new life in Christ is the closest we will ever be to the center of the universe. But that's as close as we'll ever need to be.

7

THE BIG PICTURE

At some point in time we have to make the shift from a self-centered perspective to a God-centered perspective. You and I will not make it through the difficult things we encounter if we do not look at the big picture. There are some things we have to know about God.

It is very important to know that our little part in the scheme of life does not change God. God is the same yesterday, today and forever (Hebrews 13:8). The things we experience may not seem to be consistent with who we know God to be. But it is not about our circumstances. If we look at the big picture, we will know that whatever our personal circumstance is at the moment, no matter how rough it might be, those circumstances do not change God. In fact, God is so God, when we add him to our rough circumstances, that he changes us whether he changes the circumstances or not.

Life is a much bigger picture than what you or I go through, no matter how painful or devastating it may be. The knowledge of God for who he really is has got to be part of the bigger picture if we truly desire to move from a self-centered perspective to a God-centered point of view. Looking at God through the weight of my circumstances makes life all about me. But looking at my circumstances, no matter how tragic, through the greatness and vastness of God—who knows what he is doing, who is good, big and worthy to be praised—gives an entirely different spin on my problems.

GOD KNOWS WHAT HE'S DOING

We really have to be convinced of this truth if we want to maintain our sanity. In the midst of trials and difficulties, it is very hard to believe that God knows what he is doing. Can you imagine what Joseph was thinking when he was in the pit and the prison?

A friend of mine, Diane Reeder, wrote a book titled *A Diary of Joseph*, about her experience of watching her husband suffer the ravages of leukemia. In it, she describes a number of conversations that Joseph may have had with God.

The Thing That Cannot Happen

I watch my brothers leave me in the pit,
My mouth agape in horror.
Then they come back.
I knew they couldn't leave me here long.

Wait!
What's this?
They're selling me like a piece of meat!
The way Uncle Esau sold his birthright to my father.

Will I ever see my family again?
My mother Rachel?
My father Jacob?

This is worse than death.
I thought I would be a ruler, now I am a slave
Sold to the descendants
Of Hagar, a slave-wife.

I am falling, suffocating under the weight of
My own dreams.
They are too heavy
For me to carry.

Or perhaps
I did not
Carry them well.

How did they allow this to happen?
How did God?

Looking at the Big Picture

But the truth is, God does know what he is doing. We have to look at the big picture. When we look at our circumstances in the light of the moment, things will not make sense. But if we look at the big picture, things will make better sense. Unfortunately, the big picture is not complete when we are just looking at the moment of time in which we live.

One of the differences between humans and God is God does not live in time and space; we do. God lives outside of time. He is beyond time and above time. On the other hand, we are bound by time. We are born into time, and all of our lives are contained within a timeframe. Because of that, we often do not see the big picture.

Joseph could not see how being imprisoned in a foreign country had anything to do with what God had promised him. All he knew was that he had been sold into slavery and then been betrayed. All he could understand in the moment of time in which he lived was that he had been unfairly treated. I'm sure he had difficulty understanding why God would let such terrible things happen to him.

When my nephew Ethan Cox died from pneumonia, a complication of lupus, at the age of twenty, I had some serious doubts that God knew what he was doing. When Ethan was fifteen years old, he lived with us for eighteen months after my sister, his mother, died. He was like a son to me.

His younger sister, Amanda, was only twelve when their mother died. Ethan was the closest living person Amanda had. She had come to live with us as a junior in high school, and Ethan had come to her graduation from high school earlier that summer.

We had just taken Amanda to college for a week of freshman orientation, and her classes were to start the day after we got the word that Ethan had died. We had to go to Mandy's school to inform her. Her whole life was disrupted. I just thought it was so unfair for this, another blow, to take place. I was really hurting for my niece.

She had lost her grandmother and grandfather whom she had practically lived with while her mother was sick, so they were like parents to her as well. She moved in with my brother, and they moved several times while she lived with him. Then she had moved to Detroit to live with us. She had changed schools about four times in as many years.

She had experienced a lot of changes and challenges during her short life. As far as I was concerned, she had had enough. I did not think there was a need for more trials and tribulations in her life. I really began to think that maybe there were exceptions to the truth that God does not put on us more than we can bear (1 Corinthians 10:13).

Since I am stuck in time, I don't understand why God allowed all of this to take place in my niece's and my life. But I don't have to understand right now. In fact, I don't ever have to understand. God did not mean for me to have complete understanding about the things that happen in my life. What I need to know is that God's hand is on my niece's life and that God's purposes will be fulfilled. What I can do is pray for her to draw closer to God in her time of wilderness.

We started off this chapter talking about how God knows what he is doing. Let us just go over some other things about God. We won't go into full detail, just enough to remind us of what we already know. Most of what we'll discuss about God is not new to most of us. Many of us have heard these truths before. We may have even experienced some of these attributes in our own lives. We often need to remind ourselves about basic facts from time to time. We do forget some of the basics, especially in the midst of difficulty.

The first point is *God knows what he is doing even if we don't understand it.* A second fact about God that helps me as I think of my niece's situation is *God can take what seems bad and make good out of it.* I just have to believe that even though it may seem like an impossible task. That brings me to a third point, one we have mentioned earlier: *God's ways and thoughts are not like ours.* They are different.

While I'm thinking one way about this situation, God does not think like I do. He has a different way of thinking. Not only is it impossible to figure God out, it is impossible to figure why God allows certain things. God thinks differently from us. God has all wisdom. The task is for us to come up to his way of thinking and doing so we can walk in his purposes. If we begin to walk in the fear of the Lord, we can walk in the authority given to us over the enemy.

STOP TRYING TO FIGURE GOD OUT

We can't figure God out, and that's why God has told us not to even try.

In Proverbs 3:5-6, we are instructed to lean not on our own understanding. Think about it. If we could figure God out, he wouldn't be God. If we could figure God out, we wouldn't need God. It's impossible to figure God out. God is past finding out. That's the nature of being God. We are humans, finite creations of God.

I once got a call from one of my best friends. Brenda was calling me, among other reasons, to ask for prayer for wisdom in a disappointing situation in which she found herself. She ended the call with, "The Lord has impressed on my heart and continues to remind me that I need to trust him and not lean on my own understanding. I tend to get frustrated when things don't go quite as I would like or as I predicted. But the Lord has been faithful, and I want to be faithful in my trust in him."

This is the Word for today. God is saying to each of us. "Don't lean on your own understanding. Trust me." It's hard. I'm an inquisitive person, and my mind will just go on and on trying to make sense of whatever is happening, whether good or bad.

Recently I spent lots of time thinking and trying to figure out the "whys" and "hows" of a new friendship God had brought into my life. In my line of reasoning, I already had enough friends. Why couldn't I just accept it as a gift from God and go on instead of being stuck with trying to understand it?

We spend so much time thinking instead of trusting. I have found myself saying to God a lot lately, "God, I believe. Help my unbelief." I want to experience the rest that comes from knowing God knows what he is doing.

I may not think like God and I certainly would not do it God's way, but he's God and I'm not. One of the first things he instructed us, as humans, to do was to cease trying to figure out good and evil. That brings us to the fourth point about God: *God does not want us to define good and evil.* That was the first instruction given to Adam in the garden. Eating of the tree of the knowledge of good and evil would give Adam the ability to know about good and evil apart from God. God never wanted that for his children. He wanted us to always be dependent on him as the one who would define good and bad for us. He did not want us to be like him, knowing what was good and bad. He wanted us to let him be God.

Adam and Eve blew it when they ate of the tree of the knowledge of good and evil. Although Christ has redeemed us, we still live with the desire to define good and evil on our own. Some of us may think that getting a promotion on the job is good. But if it keeps us from the things that matter the most in life—our family, our friends and God—is it really good or bad? Yes, we may be able to afford the new car and the new house, but are our lives really that much more fulfilled?

On the other hand, a job that is over our head may appear to be bad. We wonder why we ever took this job, but it causes us to seriously depend on God. It takes our life with God to a whole new level. This happened to my brother Tim. He was appointed to a state job that required him to pray and seek the Lord like he had never done before. God was faithful and gave him what he needed, but oh, did he grow spiritually during the duration of that job. From a natural point of view, the job was bad. But from God's point of view, the job was good. Similarly, a job that I hated and wanted to leave helped prepare me for what I'm doing today.

At this point, I don't know what good will come out of what my niece has gone through, but it will eventually come forth. I need to remember three more facts about God: *God is love. God is bigger than the devil. God is God all by himself and does not need my help being God.* I must keep in mind that God made my niece and he is able to keep her. He has already purchased her from the enemy. No matter what the enemy might do to try to capitalize on what she has gone through, God is able to recycle any trash the enemy puts on her and preserve the purposes that he has ordained for her. In spite of everything, the bottom line is, *God is a good God and he is worthy to be praised.*

Now having said all of that, I have to confess that I did not always praise God when I thought about the situation with my niece. Yes, I got upset with God. It really messed with my mind. I struggled big time. Some of you reading this can identify with what I'm saying. But others may be in a state of shock, wondering how I can call myself a Christian and get upset with God like that.

THE BIGGER PICTURE

I'm not proud to have to admit that I didn't have it all together, but it's the truth. Truth will bring freedom. I hope by telling the truth on myself that you, too, will be free to admit what might be in your heart about God. I trust, as you relate to what I've gone through and the events in the other people's lives that we talk about, that you too will begin to let go of your need to understand what is currently happening. And that you will realize this is part of a bigger picture and begin to understand a little more that it really is not about you.

God has a bigger picture that he is casting. Your part is just a split second in a three-hour movie. It is impossible to see how that "one second" relates to the big picture until you look back on it when it's over. For now, believe that God, the master producer, knows what he is doing. He's not trapped in time as we are. He loves you and his counsel will stand (Proverbs 19:21).

In order to understand the bigger picture, we do need to review from time to time that it's God who it really is all about. Below is a summary of some facts, among many others, that we have shared in this chapter about God, the producer of the bigger picture.

GOD

- knows what he's doing (1 Corinthians 2:6-9; Job 41:11)
- can turn bad into good (Romans 8:28; 2 Corinthians 4:7-15; 12:8-10)
- is different from us (Isaiah 55:8-10; 1 Corinthians 2:14; Proverbs 3:5-6)
- does not want us to define good and evil (Genesis 2:17; Proverbs 3:5-6)
- is love (1 John 4:8; Romans 8:32)
- is bigger than the devil (1 John 4:4)
- does not need our help (Psalm 90:2; Colossians 1:17; Jeremiah 10:6; Isaiah 46:10)
- is big (Isaiah 40:12-15, 22, 25-28)
- made us and owns us (Psalm 24:1; 100:3)
- is able to keep us (2 Timothy 1:12; Ephesians 3:20; Jude 24)
- redeemed us from the enemy (1 Corinthians 6:20; 7:23)

- is good (Psalm 86:5; 100:5)
- is worthy to be praised (Revelation 4:11; 5:12-14; Psalm 18:3)

When we move away from thinking it is about us, it becomes more and more natural to worship God even in the midst of devastating news. A friend told me that unlike her past responses to bad news, her current response to recent life-changing, disruptive circumstances has been to worship God. Even though this is one of the hardest things she has had to go through, the difference is knowing God through past experiences. Over breakfast she told me, "You know with all that I've been through [she has been through a lot] God has always been faithful."

With my niece, with my friend and with what you're going through, the big picture remains steadfast and consistent. It's not about you. The big picture is that God is a good God. That's reason enough to worship him.

8

CLOSE TO GOD

Wₑ have said more than once that in order to come into God's purpose and destiny, we have to change some thought patterns. We've got to change our ways. We might not know at this point what needs to be changed, but God is able to expose the wrong thinking. In fact, if we deliberately ask him to, God is more than willing to answer the prayer to expose whatever deceptions exist in our mind.

As you continue to read this book, I ask you to bring your heart before the Lord and say, "Just show me truth, Lord. I am willing to take whatever you show me Lord." Determine in your spirit that you will not resist truth. I pray that you will want to know what it is that hinders you from being close to God.

Are you willing to pull down any stronghold that is identified? Are you willing to let go of any lie that is exposed? If your attitude is, "I don't want to hold onto anything, Lord. I don't want to be in pride. I don't want to resist your will," then you are in the right position.

Sometimes we sing songs about how much we want to be close to God. And I think, for many of us, that's our heart's desire. We long to be close to the Lord. I was speaking at a women's conference once, and we were singing a song in which we were telling the Lord we wanted to be close to him. I was to get up and speak after we finished the song. As we were singing, the Lord impressed on me that even more than we want to be close to God, he desperately wants to be close to us. God's desire is to be close to us.

WHY ARE SO MANY OF US GOING THROUGH?

For the African American Christian woman, being close to God is not an option. In order for women to walk in divine destiny, we need to get and stay close to God. It is no secret that many women are going through. In just a few days time, I can talk to or hear from a half dozen women who are facing major obstacles in different areas of their lives.

People go through challenges from time to time, but I am amazed at how many of us are going through difficult situations all at the same time. The situations I've encountered recently ranged from relationship issues to the possibility of losing a custom-designed and built house due to strange circumstances.

In fact, this is really the time for the strange and weird to happen. I was just talking to someone, and she mentioned a very peculiar thing that had recently happened to her. She had interviewed for a job. She thought the interview had gone well. Later she found out that the person who had conducted the interview stated that she (my friend) was drunk during the interview. The person even went so far as to say that she was so convinced of this "fact" that no amount of persuasion would change her mind. My friend does not even drink, so a claim that she had been drunk in an interview was ludicrous. It was so far from the truth it was not even funny. My friend was puzzled by the accusation. She could not believe what had taken place. The situation was very strange.

We are truly living in a time in which many things do not make sense. I have talked to other people who have told me about heart-wrenching, bizarre and difficult things that are happening or have recently happened in their lives. This is the time to get close to God. We won't make it on our own. God wants women to be so close that his power in them and through them will bring victory over Satan.

I am convinced that we are entering into a time of increased spiritual activity that is unlike anything we have ever known. If we expect to make it by depending on our past experiences, we may end up being one of the casualties. Scripture tells us about the last days being times of increased deception: "Now the Spirit expressly says that in latter times some will depart from the faith, giving heed to deceiving spirits and doctrines of demons" (1 Timothy 4:1).

To be close to God is not just a good thing to strive for, it may be a matter of life or death. It may be the determining factor in surviving spiritually or going under, overtaken by a trap of the enemy. It might appear nice for us to tell God we want to be close to him. But God wants to be close to us for our safety and sanity's sake.

Now in order to defeat Satan, we've got to have God on our side. We've got to be close to God, and God's got to be close to us.

GOD WANTS TO BE CLOSE TO US

God wants to get next to us. God wants to be all up in our business. There are some things he wants to do in our lives, such as healing and restoring us. To do these, he must come close.

God knows there are some things that need to be rooted out of our lives. There are things in our lives that need to be thrown down and destroyed in order for God to be close to us (Jeremiah 1:10). We often have ways of thinking that are a deterrent to God's nearness. The common mindset of American women hinders God from being close to us. In fact, there are times when God tries to come close to us and we push him back.

We don't always understand God's ways. God's ways and thoughts are higher than ours; how can we walk together with God unless our ways and thoughts are in agreement with his? (Isaiah 55:8; Amos 3:3) Somebody has to make an adjustment. Somebody has to change.

If God has higher thoughts and higher ways, then in order for us to be close, to walk together, we have to bring our ways and thoughts up to his higher level. Our ways and thoughts—yes, even the traditional ways and thoughts of SBWs—have been down on a lower plane. But if we desire to walk together with the Lord, if we want to be close, then we have to make up our mind that we are the ones who will bring it up to the higher level. We've got to think and act on a higher perspective than the self-centered one we are accustomed to.

God is not going to come walk with us. He's inviting us to come walk with him. Walking with him, in his ways, means if somebody persecutes you, you pray for them. It means when it's tight and it's tough and it's hard, you say, "Great, now God's strength is made perfect in my weakness."

I have been the one who has had to change as I have learned to walk with God in his purposes for me. Believe me, it's a big waste of time trying to get God to change. But if we can agree to be the ones who will make the changes, of course by God's grace, we can be powerful change agents in God's hands. I am still changing as I seek to enter further into his rest.

HINDRANCES TO CLOSENESS

You will not be a woman who knows God and is able to hear him clearly if you do not throw out pride and resistance. Those are the things that hinder us. Pride will keep us from the truth. Too many times we use the excuse, "Well that's what I always thought," or "That's how I've always been." However, God is saying, "It's time to think my thoughts. It's time to move on up to my plans and purposes."

God must be tired of seeing his enemy mess over his people. I know I'm tired of being messed over. I bet you are too. God loves us. He wants to rescue us. He longs to bring us away and out of the enemy's plans. He desires to teach us his ways.

> He made known His ways to Moses,
> His acts to the children of Israel. (Psalm 103:7)

Moses knew the ways of God. The children of Israel only knew his acts. A lot of us know about the acts of God, we know of God's provisions and blessings. We know his acts, but we do not know his ways.

God invited Moses and all of the children of Israel to come close to him. He gave an invitation to everyone. He told them how to prepare themselves, "Cleanse yourself three days, and then I'm going to come and meet with you. I'm going to come and talk to you. Come nigh, come close to me." And God came close. There was thunder, there was lightening, and He began to speak. Read the account in Exodus 19:7-25 and Exodus 20:18-21.

When God came close, God's people were afraid and ran away. They couldn't take the magnitude of God's presence. They could not handle God being that close to them. So they told Moses, "You talk to God. You get what he wants to tell you. Then you come and tell us. We'll listen to you and do what he says. We just don't want to hear God for ourselves." The same thing is happening today. We pay people to hear from God. We go to listen to what they've heard, but few of us seek to hear from God ourselves.

God wanted to be close to all of his people, not just Moses. He invited them to come close to him. When he came close, they fled. Only Moses drew close. Why? Moses knew about the ways of God, not just his acts. Moses asked to see God's glory (Exodus 33:18). That's why he could handle God's presence.

THE ACTS OF GOD

The acts of God are what happen down here in the physical realm, so when we get the promotion on our job, that's an act of God. And we think, "Oh God is good." Now we say he's good because we got a raise or we received a promotion. When we get healed from physical ailments, God is good. These are acts of God.

In the beginning of this book, I told you of being at death's door with little hope of living and the possibility of being paralyzed and in a vegetative state if I were to live. There is no doubt that an act of God is behind the fact that I am alive some thirty years later. I have experienced God's healing power on other occasions as well.

I have also experienced God's miraculous provision in my life. Many of us can testify of a divine component operating in areas of our lives. There was one job I was offered that had a divine signature all over it—from the way I found out about the job to the type of job. It was as if the job was tailor-made for me. Maybe getting a job is an ordinary function of life, but this time I could see that it was an act of God.

Many of us have experienced God's acts in some way or another. Once a lady was led to a particular house. When she got to the door, someone called out to tell her that the door was open, "Come in. I've been waiting for you." She had never seen the woman before, never been to her house, but that day God directed her there. She went in and prayed for her. She found out later that this sick woman had recovered. In fact, she later discovered that the woman's daughter actually worked at the same job where she worked, and she was able to find out about her on a regular basis. Now that is an act of God. God demonstrated his healing ability through one of his children to another of his children. He did it in a miraculous way, as well. God's hand was all over this event in the sick woman's life.

Experiencing God in miraculous ways is truly a blessing. One of the ladies in my discipleship group experienced one of those miraculous blessings from God. The IRS was auditing her. She's a hairdresser and the lady she paid her booth rental fee to for years did not want to cooperate and supply some of the information she needed for the audit. The situation didn't look good. She was almost certain she was going to have to pay a lot of fines. I remember talking to her on the phone about it several times. She was really worried.

She called me the other day to tell me the case had been thrown out. Boy, was she praising God for his goodness when she called me; she was shouting on the phone! She had experienced an act of God. She found out that God was bigger than the IRS.

We had a similar experience with the IRS. I too was worried. They said we owed $6,000. Well, God came through for us as well. In fact, because of the audit, we found more receipts that had not been accounted for, and the IRS ended up giving us a check for an additional $300.

THE WAYS OF GOD VERSUS THE ACTS OF GOD

We often evaluate God's goodness based on his acts. However, God's ways also encompass his goodness, but his ways are different. In order to help you to comprehend his ways, God may have to withdraw his acts. Sometimes God will seemingly withdraw his presence. This is where it gets tricky. It may begin to appear that God is not so good when some of his acts are withheld.

It is very important to separate God from his acts. If something happens in our life that we would define as "bad," that does not change the nature of God. Why is it that we define God based on what happens to us on a daily basis? God is not confined to time. What we experience in time can never be the basis for defining God. God's goodness remains even when we don't see it being manifested in our life.

When "bad" things happen, we act confused, schizophrenic. In our mind, we think, "God is good." In our emotions, we think, "No, he's not good." A double-minded man is unstable in all his ways (James 1:8). What God wants to do is to bring your level of thinking up to where you understand his ways and his thoughts.

GOD'S WAYS CONCENTRATE ON THE INTERIOR

Do you know that God is most interested in conforming you to his image? Did you know that according to the ways of God, he will actually allow you to stay in a situation longer than you think is good? Sometimes God is more interested in building your character than in making you comfortable. God is determined to take you through rather than get you out of your situation.

For instance, maybe you have a job that you hate. You have to supervise some mean and ornery workers. You want to get away from that job as soon as possible. You've been praying, crying, fasting and interviewing for other positions. You have your whole church praying for you. You even called prayer hotlines around the country, including TBN and *The 700 Club*. Everybody is praying for you to get another job, but it doesn't happen.

As far as you're concerned, you cannot make it another day. Yet the heavens are like a brick wall where it concerns God answering your prayer about another job. Years later, you look back on that experience and realize how God used that job as a springboard to get you to where you are today. Today you couldn't be happier. Yet without that particular job and what you learned while hating every minute of it, you wouldn't be where you are today. Today you can thank God for *not* answering your prayer back then to let you get another job. Perhaps it was management skills you would need to run your own company. Maybe it was people skills. Maybe it was perseverance.

In order to work patience, character or unconditional love in you, God will allow you to stay in a situation longer than you thought was possible. God is more interested in building you up in the image of Christ than he is in making you comfortable.

RUNNING FROM GOD

Why do we run? Why do we run when God begins to come close? Why do you and I run? We run because God is light and a consuming fire (1 John 1:5; Hebrews 12:29). When God begins to draw close to us, He will begin to expose dark areas of our lives. He'll begin to burn off the unpurified parts of our lives. When that happens, we hurt. Because of the pain, we draw back. We don't like pain. I know I don't.

Another reason we run from God is because of pride. We don't like to admit that there is anything in our life that should not be there. We may be deceived about how mature we are in God. It's really tricky when we have been Christians for a long time. It is especially difficult to admit that there are areas of our lives that need to change when our background includes growing up in a Christian family, such as mine.

Maybe we did not become a Christian at a young age, but we are very active in religious activity. We may have served in the missionary societies, acted as chairperson of the women's day committee, worked in the nurse's guild or taught VBS, Bible classes, Sunday school and a whole host of other things. We may even be in ministry.

However, when the rubber meets the road—and it has in the road of my life a number of times—you will find out that all of your religious activity really isn't getting it. Sometimes our activity is a big façade, a cover for what we are really not. Perhaps you will find there is hate, bitterness or some other junk in you that you didn't know was there. You had effectively covered it up all these years. But when a situation or a trial comes, the junk shows up.

Once God begins to expose the junk in us, we draw back from him. We fear what people will think about us when they see the junk. How can we admit to petty things in our lives that should have been dealt with a long time ago? How can we acknowledge a spirit of jealousy in us after all these years? Where did the anger, anxiety and fear come from?

Sometimes, we don't even admit to the things God is trying to show us. We run and hide. We don't want others to see our junk, but neither do we want to see it ourselves.

We throw the stuff back under the rug. We think to ourselves, "No, that's not me." We'll blame it on just having a bad hair day, or we'll blame someone else—our parents, our children, our boss, the dog, whatever.

Like many of us, King Saul succumbed to pride and fear of the people rather than allowing the fear of God to keep him from being disobedient to God (1 Samuel 15). On top of that, Saul became self-deceived. He really thought he had done all God had told him. Many times, we have no idea how far away our lives are from God. We, too, can be self-deceived. That's why it is important for us to go to God and ask him to give us his verdict on our hearts and lives.

The proof of our walk with God is the life of God in us—the life, the active character of God and the unconditional love of God operating in us. When the fear of God is in us, that's the sign of maturity. God comes close to touch unhealed areas. God comes close to purify and to restore. Yet when we draw back or run, we are not exhibiting the fear of God. We shouldn't fear what people are going to say. We shouldn't even fear what we're going to find out about ourselves. God wants us to fear him alone.

Do You Want God to Talk with You?

God is saying, "I want to talk. I want to get to know you. I want you to get to know me. Let's get some of this stuff out on the table and deal with it so that we can get close. If we don't deal with it, there will always be distance. When we don't deal with it, you'll have this problem with trust in me. If you don't trust me, then you're not going to obey me."

Some of us are not sure if we can trust God. We remember the times he didn't seem to come through for us in the past, so we think we have to provide our own protection. We become determined to take care of ourselves. We build walls for protection. These walls keep us from getting close to God, and they keep us away from others. If God could just talk some things over with us, we would find out some things about God. We would find out some things about our past circumstances. We would find out that Satan was behind a lot of the junk in the past.

When things happen we don't understand, we should draw close to God to gain insight instead of running away. We are God's co-laborers and partners; it's about God, not us. We can stop looking at things from a self-centered perspective. Instead of complaining and wondering, "What about me?" perhaps we should ask, "What is this really about?" Maybe we'll begin to ask, "What about God?" We must begin to be concerned about what God is trying to do in this. We need to attune ourselves to his agenda.

As we draw close to God, getting back into his lap, we can turn to face the enemy and tell him to leave us alone. Be assured that when Satan sees that we've drawn near to God, he'll flee (James 4:7-8).

GOD IS IN THE BUSINESS OF RADICAL CHANGE

I believe that the fate of this country hinges on the people of God who know the presence of God. African American Christian women are members of the body of Christ that make up a critical portion of the people who live in urban areas, areas that at first glance seem to be overtaken by evil. Therefore, I believe the fate of many of the cities in America will be directly related to the number of African American Christian women who draw close to God.

If we desire to be part of a people who are available to God to do great exploits and demonstrate victory, then we have to know God better. The fate of our urban areas could lie on African American women knowing their God. "The people who know their God shall be strong, and carry out great exploits" (Daniel 11:32).

God wants to do a work in you that the world has never seen. Everyone will say this is the Lord's doing and it is marvelous in our eyes (Matthew 21:42). God will do a work in us so that people will come running to us because they'll see something in us that will make them ask us about God.

It all begins when we refuse to run away from God when we are in pain. Instead, we choose to draw close. Or perhaps, we did run away, but we came to our senses and came back home. God wants to erase the lies and get rid of deception. It's time to get close to God. What's on your mind right now that hinders you from getting close to God?

TOUGH, NAGGING OR UNANSWERED QUESTIONS

Many of us have questions about something that happened in the past. Those unanswered questions sometimes hinder us from getting close to God. If you have identified something that is keeping you away from God, acknowledge it as a potential problem and put it on the shelf. Don't let an unanswered question keep you stuck.

God will deal with the questions at an appropriate time. But don't stay away from him because of unanswered questions. Some of us have done that far too long. Every time God wants to come close, these questions come up in our mind or emotions. Then we get stuck. There are a lot of things that we will understand better by and by. We just need to put those things on the shelf for the time being. God wants to know if we will trust him, sight unseen.

God is ready to get close to us. God wants to get close to us more than we want to get close to him. Are there some things that you throw in his face when he tries to draw nigh? Are there things that keep you from drawing nigh to him? Is there some pain, some hurt, some abuse?

Are there things that happened in the past, but the resulting bitterness and unforgiveness still remain? Every time you think about that situation, it just irks you. You can't get past it. You can't understand how God allowed it to happen. You think, "If God is really so good, why didn't he do something? If he's really as in control as he wants us to believe he is, he could've stopped it."

God is saying, "You want to draw near to me. I want to draw near to you. Would you do something for me? Would you put that on the shelf for now? Could you stop allowing that to keep you from me?"

God is saying, "I love you." Can you trust me with your pain? Can you admit it hurts a lot? There's still some hurt there now. Can you allow me by the power and presence of my Holy Spirit to touch you? I'm the God of all comfort. Can you allow me to soothe it? Can you allow my love for you to touch you? I feel the hurt more acutely than you feel it."

God is working on us, trying to build us. God is trying to make us into Spirit-filled, Spirit-led women. It's not about us. God has chosen us. God is unable to do what he wants to do in this world until you and I are totally convinced that he loves us immensely. We need to comprehend we've been chosen for a destiny and purpose. We need to be assured that God's power is available for us to accomplish all his plans, his will and his purposes. It's not *about* us, but it is *up* to us.

We are to be co-laborers and partners with God, not co-gods. We are to be surrendered vessels, willing to do what he commands. It's really very simple. We just need to see things from his perspective.

9

GOD'S IDENTITY

To change from living in the strength that comes from our own efforts to living in newness of life is still a very difficult, even impossible, lesson for many strong black women. But the change is necessary if we are going to walk close to God and be used by him as keys to change. If we are new creations in Christ, we are not what we used to be. This chapter will examine what it means to live in our new identity.

We are not what we were before Christ. We are new creations. We may not look different, we may not feel different, we may not act different, but we are different. The Word of God tells us that we are to walk by faith, not by sight. We call ourselves people of the Word, people of faith, women who love and obey God; yet many of us, including yours truly, simply refuse to walk a new way because it is not comfortable for us. We refuse to trust God with every aspect of our lives unless we can understand exactly what God is doing, how he is doing it and how long he will take to get it done. That process takes us into areas of discomfort.

Once we get the basic knowledge that our personal comfort is not as high on God's agenda as manifesting the life of his Son through our lives, we'll probably move along much quicker. When we are self-centered and self-focused, our personal comfort is high on *our* list of priorities.

But when our lives are God focused, then what is really important to God will be a concern for us as well. If we are seeking him first, we'll be more prone to cooperate with God in the purposes he has for us. We will be less apt to pull back when we go through the uncomfortable times.

Many of us could handle the difficult things we go through if a few things about the purpose were explained to us. We can go through almost anything as long as we buy into the rationale. So let me make it clear. God's purpose for working death in us is to get to the treasure. God wants us to live in our spiritual identity. However, as we are going through, we cannot expect to know what and when things will take place. If we knew everything, we would not need to walk by faith. Walking with God takes faith. As we get to know God, our faith increases.

God's task for all of his children is that we move on up, grow up spiritually. Why is it that we get stuck? Many of us do not know that we are new. Many of us really do not understand what happened to us at the new birth. For many of us, we are stuck in how or what we were before becoming a Christian.

THIS WAS YOUR LIFE

It is good to review who you were before coming to know God. We all have been born at least once. Our first birth was of the flesh. Before you were born again, you were dead to God according to Ephesians 2:

> And you He made alive, who were dead in trespasses and sins, in which you once walked according to the course of this world, according to the prince of the power of the air, the spirit who now works in the sons of disobedience, among whom also we all once conducted ourselves in the lusts of our flesh, fulfilling the desires of the flesh and of the mind, and were by nature children of wrath, just as the others. But God, who is rich in mercy, because of His great love with which He loved us, even when we were dead in trespasses, made us alive together with Christ (by grace you have been saved). (Ephesians 2:1-5)

Before we were born again, we were slaves to sin. We couldn't do right; we had no power or ability to do right. We were chained to sin. We may have wanted to do right but we couldn't. The Scripture passage above tells us we were not only dead in our sins but were living our lives to fulfill fleshly desires.

Bound to sin is what all of us were before being born again. Before being born again, Satan was our father. We had no spiritual discernment, no love and no Word in us. Whatever might have been in our old nature—be it lying, stealing, immorality, people-pleasing, selfishness, pride or hatred—was the basis of our old identity. Before Christ, we may have been very hard. Perhaps we carried a chip on our shoulder. We may have been very bitter about the things that happened in our life. We may have carried around a lot of anger. People may have wanted to avoid crossing our path.

Unfortunately some of us look and act like the same people we were before Christ. But God says we are new. We should be acting different. If we have been born again, we are not the same as we were before.

BORN AGAIN

Everyone can have a second birth. While the first birth is of the flesh, the second birth is of the Spirit (John 3:5). Now if you've been born of the Spirit, you receive an entirely new life. God's Spirit came into your human spirit and gave you his power. You are no longer a child of Satan, following the dictates of the flesh, but you are a child of God. And you are free to follow God.

If we had only experienced the first birth, we would be spiritually dead. That means we would be separated from God. In the second birth, we were made alive together with Christ. We have been raised up together and made to sit in heavenly places together with Christ (Ephesians 2:5-6). This is our new identity. We are new creations in Christ. All of the old is gone (1 Corinthians 5:17).

The Word of God is clear on the fact that we are new and that we have a new life within us. One main reason we have not changed is because we still remember what it used to be like when we were dead. We have not fully grasped what we now have in Christ because of the memory of what it was like before Christ. God made a whole new person in our spirit, but he did not wipe out our memory.

We can still remember everything about our life before Christ. We remember how we used to protect ourselves. Instead of acting out of our new identity, which is seated with Christ in heaven, we go with the memory of our old. We remember how we used to get our needs met before we came to Christ. When God tells us to do something that is opposite of how we used to do things, we are apt to disregard what God says to us and go with how we have always done it. We still remember how it used to be. Our minds are not renewed.

We have everything we need to live as new creations in Christ, but when we don't know what we have, our lives will still reflect our old identity. We are told in 2 Peter that God's divine power has given us everything we need to be godly.

> As His divine power has given to us all things that pertain to life and godliness, through the knowledge of Him who called us by glory and virtue, by which have been given to us exceedingly great and precious promises, that through these you may be partakers of the divine nature, having escaped the corruption that is in the world through lust. (2 Peter 1:3-4)

The key word in this passage is *knowledge*. The reason we don't live in all we have is we don't have a proper knowledge of our new identity. Our new identity is the identity of God. Living in this new identity kills the old identity, the way we are used to doing it. It puts to death the flesh. But the truth is that our old nature is supposed to be dead anyway. When you are in Christ, the old you is crucified.

We are new creations, but we don't venture to live in our new identity as long as the memory of the old is still so strong. So our task is to grow in grace and knowledge of the new life placed within us. As we grow in the knowledge of our new identity and walk in that new life by faith, we change into the likeness of Christ.

The key is walking in our new identity through trusting and obeying God. It's not just mental knowledge. We can sit in church for years, getting our minds filled with Scripture and having all kinds of emotional experiences, but never learning to walk in the newness of life made available to us.

Some people think or say, "That's just the way I am." No, that's the way you remembered it to be. That's not the way you are because you are a new creation. Old things are passed away and all things have become new (2 Corinthians 5:17). The Holy Spirit, the same Spirit that raised Jesus from the dead, now lives in your mortal body (Romans 8:11). You can do what he tells you to do because you have God's Spirit working through you. You don't have an old sinful nature, but you have a flesh that retains the memory of the old. The old you was put to death on the cross.

It is often taught that we have two natures. We are told to stop feeding the old and let the new nature grow. *I do not believe the believer has two natures.* We have a divine nature. It is not a struggle with an old nature. The old is dead. The old has passed away. Let's just get that straight once and for all. Your problem is not a sinful nature if you are a Christian. As a Christian, you have a divine nature.

Paul was very explicit in Romans 6 in letting us know that the old has been crucified. It was a strange prospect for Paul that Christians who had died to sin would continue to live in it.

> How shall we who died to sin live any longer in it? Or do you not know that as many of us as were baptized into Christ Jesus were baptized into His death? Therefore we were buried with Him through baptism into death, that just as Christ was raised from the dead by the glory of the Father, even so we also should walk in newness of life. For if we have been united together in the likeness of His death, certainly we also shall be in the likeness of His resurrection, knowing this, that our old man was crucified with Him, that the body of sin might be done away with, that we should no longer be slaves of sin. For he who has died has been freed from sin. Now if we died with Christ, we believe that we shall also live with Him. (Romans 6:2-8)

So we don't have an old sin nature to deal with, but we do have a problem. In fact, Galatians 5:16 tells us to walk in the Spirit, in God's identity, and we will not fulfill the lusts of the flesh. The problem is we have a choice; we can choose to live in the new nature or the memory of the old. The old is gone, but we still remember it and we can choose to live out of that memory.

The Word of God does speak of a fight that goes on within our being; it's the fight of the flesh against the spirit. The fight of the flesh versus the Spirit is a struggle between the memory of the old rather than an old nature. Perhaps it is only semantics, but I think we have a lot more hope if we realize our difficulty is one of having the memory of something now dead, instead of having a nature that is yet alive within us. To fight the memory, we can choose to remember new facts (unseen spiritual realities).

Remember the analogy of the telephone remembering how it was used by the old occupant, and thus it was not comfortable with the way the new owner wanted to use it? When we're used to using our mouths to tell people off, we will not be comfortable using our mouths to say nice things or pray for others. Or if, like me, we are used to using our personality to withdraw from those we love, coming close to them in a time of misunderstanding is not natural. It will be very uncomfortable because it is a new way of thinking and doing.

THE FEDERAL WITNESS PROTECTION SYSTEM

Let me give an illustration that describes our problem. When someone has been a witness on a federal case that would endanger their life, the government will put them in a program called "Witness Protection." In the program, the person gets a whole new identity. They get a new name, a new social security number and a new birth certificate. They are given a new place to live. The government can legally do this.

When someone becomes a Christian, Jesus says, "I am taking you out of the kingdom of darkness and putting you in the kingdom of light. I am giving you a whole new identity. You are not a sinner anymore. You are a saint. I'm giving you a new name, a new address and a new social security number. You get a new birth certificate. You are born again. You have a whole new identity. It's all legal." God can do that. God can give you his identity. God gives you a new citizenship.

So let's imagine the person who needs to go into the witness protection program is named Harold Guy. Harold lives in Memphis, Tennessee. After getting into the federal program, his legal name will now become Ronald Taylor. At birth, he was given the name Harold Guy, but the government makes him a new birth certificate with the name Ronald Taylor.

Ronald gets a new social security number. The government gives him a home in a new city. He now lives in Houston, Texas, with his wife, Sharon. The government agents work with Ronald. They tell Ronald he should never answer to the name Harold Guy ever again in his life. He needs to forget he ever was Harold. This is extremely important. His very life could be in danger if he answers to his old name.

The agents sit down with him and school him on his new identity. They have even made up a new extended family for him. They have covered all of the tracks so that the people he testified against can't come after him.

The agents continue to work with Ronald. Sometimes they call him on the phone and ask for Harold just to see if he will respond. Sometimes they see him on the street and call out, "Harold." Just testing.

In the beginning, he almost answers to Harold, but then he remembers, *No, I'm Ronald.* He walks around practicing, "I'm Ronald. I'm Ronald. I'm Ronald."

Legally he is Ronald, but he still remembers being Harold. Ronald's problem is not two identities or two natures. He is solely Ronald, but it's hard to erase all of the memory of being Harold. He had been Harold for forty years and Ronald for only six months. Unfortunately, Ronald remembers more of Harold than he does of Ronald.

His adversaries are banking on being able to trip Ronald up because of his memory of his identity as Harold. They have no idea what his new name is. They only know the old name. So when they look for him, they can only use the old name, hoping Ronald will respond out of his memory and answer. They are looking for Harold because he put their comrade in jail for life. They want revenge. They want to kill him if possible.

When the federal agents were trying to help Ronald, a few times, he almost slipped. Now he is on his own. If he slips when his adversaries catch up with him, he could lose his life. Every morning, Ronald has to tell himself, "I'm Ronald." He has to soak in the knowledge of his new identity. He's got to know it. He's got to memorize it. He's got to think about his new identity all the time. He cannot afford to live out of the memory of the old.

GOD'S PROTECTION PROGRAM

When each of us was born the first time, we were born with the name "sinner." We demonstrated our identity in various ways—perhaps as a liar, gossiper, adulterer or hater. When you became a Christian, you received a totally new name, a new identity. Your name is no longer "sinner," and you are no longer a liar, gossiper, worrier, adulterer or hater. You may have told the biggest mess of lies yesterday, but today as a Christian, you are a new creation. God has given you a totally new identity. God's Holy Spirit lives within you.

The adversary of every Christian remembers all of our old ways. If a person was a gossiper, a slanderer, a liar or a worrier, then that's what the enemy will use to call out to them. He's using the old identity. If he can get you to remember who you used to be and act out of that memory, he can get his claws back into you.

You also remember how you used to be. So when you're walking down the street, the enemy is going to whisper, "Gossiper, fornicator, liar, worrier." Sometimes we respond and say, "You talking to me?" But what we need to do when we hear our old name is to keep walking, saying, "I'm a saint. I'm a saint. I'm a saint." It's not about the old you, it's about the new you—the you who is now in Christ and who Christ dwells in.

You've got to know your new identity—who you are in Christ—and you've got to forget the old. If you remember the old, you'll walk in it. That's why the Word of God says, "Grow in the grace and knowledge of our Lord and Savior Jesus Christ" (2 Peter 3:18). You need to grow in grace and knowledge of who he is in you and who you are in him. When you grow in that knowledge, you will stop answering to "sinner."

You will say, "No, That's not me anymore. I'm free; I don't have to answer to that name. That person is dead. Yes, I spent twenty years gossiping. But I'm a new creation. I'm free not to gossip anymore. I'm free to bless people.

Perhaps you could say, "Before I became a Christian, I spent many years as a liar, thief, slanderer and many of the other names for a sinner, but now I am a new creation. I used to walk in that old way as if I had a ball and chain on my feet. But with Christ in me now, the chains are broken. I don't have to keep dragging my legs just because I walked that way for twenty-five years. I'm free. I can run. It doesn't matter if I've only been free to run for three months and I've walked for twenty years dragging a ball and chain.

"Yes, sometimes I get up in the morning and, out of habit, I drag my right leg, but then I look down and remember that I don't have to walk that way anymore. I have been set free. There are no more chains holding me."

Paul tells the Galatians to stand in the liberty wherein Christ has set them free. He instructs them not to be entangled again with a yoke of bondage (Galatians 5:1). It is possible to be free and to get entangled again. We get off course because we continue to walk out of our mind and our will and our emotions (our memory of the old nature) instead of walking in the new (the Spirit).

Choosing to Walk in the Spirit

Remember, we don't have an old nature that has to sin. We have a flesh that lusts against the Spirit. You have a mind, a will and emotions that remember how it used to be. And so when you choose to walk based on your memory and when you choose to walk based on how you understand things, you will walk in the flesh. But when you choose to walk in your new identity in Christ, your new power, your new strength and your new life, you will walk in the Spirit.

But it hurts to walk in the Spirit because it kills everything you used to be. But that's why the Word of God says, "Likewise you also, reckon yourselves to be dead indeed to sin, but alive to God in Christ Jesus our Lord" (Romans 6:11). You already have died to the old nature, so now reckon yourself dead to it. When you reckon yourself dead to sin that means when the opportunity comes to walk in the Spirit versus walking in the flesh you can say, "I'll walk in the Spirit. Even if it kills me."

And it will kill you; it will kill your understanding, your feelings and your own personal desires because walking in the Spirit takes you to a whole new level — the level of the supernatural, the level of Spirit-filled living.

There's nothing that God tells us to do in his Word that is natural for us to do. Just think about it; it's not natural to pray for those who spitefully use you, nor is it natural to overcome evil with good. It's not natural to esteem others better than ourselves. It's not natural to give thanks to God in everything. These are all characteristics of our new nature, but they are not a part of our natural tendencies.

That's why to walk in the Spirit takes the grace of God. That's one of the reasons the things we go through are so difficult. Because God is trying to bring you to the point of crying out for his grace. He's waiting for you to say, "I can't do this."

Religious Soul Strength

But the problem is we still try to do it in what I call, "religious soul strength." We think that if we can learn a few more verses, stand in another line and have another hand laid on us, get a few more spiritual experiences, get a little bit more emotion and a little bit more determination, get a demon cast out of us or a bucket of oil poured on us, then we'll be able to do this Christian thing right.

Let me say that I believe in laying on of hands, memorizing Scripture, evicting the devil and the whole nine yards. But I have also found that we make things too complicated. There is a simplicity in Christ (2 Corinthians 11:3). When we rely on anything other than Christ, what we're doing is we're still trying to strengthen the soul with religious things. We have a form of godliness, but we deny the real power thereof, which is the power of God in us to do it.

WALKING IN OUR NEW IDENTITY

What was God doing as he took you through difficulties? God was building himself in you. God was getting you to the place where you now realize you have to depend on him. You are convinced you can't make it on your own. God was changing you in the process. The tears you cried to him were changing you. They made you soft and pliable. You are not as hard now.

The waiting effected a change in you. You no longer have to have things right away. You're more patient with others. You almost grew weary in well doing, but as you waited, God took away some of the harshness.

A friend told me that when she went to the parking lot after work and saw her car window smashed, she was like, "Oh, well." She said, "I had just gotten through reading something Maya Angelou had said about how as you grow older things don't affect you like they used to. A couple of years ago I would have been so upset, but it just wasn't that big of a deal." There would be some inconvenience. There would be an additional expense, but it could be fixed, and it just was not worth getting all worked up over.

African American Christian women, let us stop remembering how we used to do it. Let us stop behaving out of the memory of the pain, rejection and abuse we have suffered. Let us grow in grace and knowledge of our Lord and Savior, Jesus Christ. It's time to let go. It's a new day. It's time for a new thing. It's time to walk in our new identity.

10

WOMEN:
GOD'S CO-LABORERS

Sometimes I wonder why in the world God uses me. When I look at me, the natural me, I'm shy, an introvert at my core. I tend to be disorganized. I misplace things. I can get easily distracted. I can be forgetful. I can be so focused on tasks that I neglect relationships. It's hard for me to speak up for me. I internalize things like anger and bitterness. I'm not always open and upfront about my feelings. Sometimes I'm not even in touch with my feelings. I have struggled with feelings of inferiority and worthlessness. I've sought comfort in food. I've battled lots of fears. I've struggled with discouragement and depression. I've found out I can be passive-aggressive. I can be stubborn. God has shown me much pride in my life. When you look at all of this, and a whole lot more besides, it appears I'm pretty messed up. Well, I am. But why would God use someone as messed up as me? It's not about me anyway. That's what we've been trying to make clear in this book.

Some people will have problems with the fact that I went into such detail concerning my shortcomings. I don't focus on these shortcomings. They are there. I've had to acknowledge them in order to die to them. My weaknesses, faults, sins, shortcomings and mistakes make up part of who I am. But thank God, his strength is perfected in my weaknesses. Thank God, the blood of Jesus washes me free from my sins. Knowing who I am without God keeps me clinging to him.

I have much strength as well. God has been good to me. He has blessed me in many ways. (I would list all of my strengths, but that would take too many pages.) God is not really upset over my weaknesses. Neither is he impressed by my strengths. It's not about who or what I am; it's about God and who and what he is in me. It doesn't really matter what weaknesses *or* strengths I have. As we learned in an earlier chapter, his strength is demonstrated the most when I am weak.

What about that long list of strengths I have? If he chooses to use my strengths, that's fine. He made me. The strengths ultimately came from him. But again, he's not impressed by my natural strengths; he gets better results from my life by being the strength in my weakness.

But let's say I choose to use the talents he gave me instead of burying them; it is still God who gives the grace and wisdom to do that. As long as I honor God, use the strengths to bring glory to him and don't get lifted up in pride, thinking like Nebuchadnezzar that I am what I am by my own hand, we'll be straight. I know that I am what I am by the grace of God (1 Corinthians 15:10).

I am somebody because Christ has chosen me as a vessel in which he dwells and through which he desires to express himself. My vessel is earthen, but the treasure is out of this world. It's not about me. It's about Christ in me. That's the hope of glory. God wants me to think soberly of myself, not too high, not too low (Romans 12:3). I know I am loved by God, not because I was good enough and not because I deserved his love. I can rest assured that he still loves me when I mess up and in spite of how messed up I may be.

Jesus loves me this I know. In spite of all the mess I am in the natural he has chosen to use me as a vessel in his hands. Perhaps in God's kingdom, the worse off you are, the more he's able to use you. God plus a mess equals a message. A messed up life plus God equals GOD. God added to anything equals GOD. The more I get all wrapped up, tied up and tangled up in Jesus, the more you see him and the less you see of my mess. That's the message he has for you. It's not about you. It's about God. When God is the source of my life, I can walk in his strength. His strength just happens to overshadow all of my weakness.

GOD USED GIDEON

One of the things God has made clear to me is his desire to use African

American women. The prophet Isaiah tells us that God's ways and thoughts are on a higher level than ours (Isaiah 55:8-10). One of the ways of God is to choose those who others overlook.

In Judges 6, God purposely chose Gideon, a man who was fearful and felt unqualified (v. 27). He claimed to be of the weakest clan and the least in his own family (v. 15). When God came to speak to Gideon, Gideon was hiding from the Midianites. Yet God chose Gideon to be the one he would use to save Israel from the Midianites. It wasn't about Gideon. It was about God who had sent him.

God wanted to make a statement that He was the one who got the job done. Why else would he purposefully choose someone who was fearful and felt unqualified?

When Gideon had 32,000 men join with him to fight against the Midianites, God wasn't satisfied. God told Gideon that the people with him were too many for him to conquer the Midianites. With that many people, the army would easily take the credit for the victory (Judges 7:2). God did not want that. He wanted it to be clear that this was a God thing. God wanted to do this. He only needed those who would be available to be tools in his hands. He wanted the whole world to know that this was the Lord's doing. God wanted to make it abundantly clear that he and he alone was responsible for the victory.

In the first round of elimination, 22,000 people went back home. There were just 10,000 left. But that still was too many for God. He really wanted to make a statement that it was not about human beings. In the second round of elimination, 9,700 did not pass, and Gideon was left with only 300 men.

God was not satisfied until he had whittled the army down to 300 soldiers. With 32,000 strong, there would have been the temptation for the men to take the credit for the victory over the enemy; but with only 300 men going against an army as numerous as locusts, it could only be God who got the victory for them.

With the strategy God gave him, Gideon and his little army eventually defeated 135,000 of their enemies. Even if Gideon had 32,000 against 135,000, we would know it wasn't about Gideon. But 300 defeating 135,000? Truly this was a supernatural occurrence—a God thing. God wanted everyone to know that it was all about God.

THE PEOPLE GOD USES

Do you want to know what kind of God our God really is? I've found out that he's the kind of God who looks around and says, "Now let's see, who are the ones who are most likely to be overlooked? Oh, it's African American women. It looks like my enemy has beaten them up. They are hurting and spiritually weak. They have low self-esteem just like Gideon. Many use their tongues in a caustic way to hurt others. Okay, then that's who I'm going to use. You see when I get through with them, and they get close to me and I get close to them, everybody will know that it's not about them. It will clearly be seen that it's about me. I'm going to get the credit and everybody will know that I am God. Everybody will be so surprised; they'll be shocked, trying to figure out how in the world did I use African American women!"

I can imagine some of the people who know us well having an argument with God over this: "Listen, God, (smiling) I've got to tell you something really funny. This friend of mine thinks you have chosen her to defeat the enemy. Ha, ha, ha. I never heard anything so funny. Why in the world would she think you wanted to use her?"

"She thinks that because that's what I've told her."

"What's that you say? I don't think I heard you clearly."

"I said I was the one who told her I had chosen her to defeat the enemy."

"Really? Wow! That is really unbelievable. Are we talking about the same person? The friend I'm talking about is stubborn and mean. Were you aware of those issues? She still has a problem with her tongue."

"And?"

"Surely you would not choose to use someone whose tongue is so sharp. Well, I mean she just doesn't have it together. She told me off just yesterday. Look at the way she . . . You know what I mean. I just imagined you would want someone who was truly seeking you. I don't know when the last time was that she really prayed, except when she was in trouble. How could she hear you speaking to her if she didn't seek you?"

"She has not chosen me. I have chosen her."

"Okay . . . but, but she doesn't know that much about the Word."

"And?"

"Well, I have a seminary degree. I've been seeking you all these years, and I have never heard you tell me what she claims you told her. If anyone was qualified to be used by you, it would be me, not her."

"Son, you don't understand my ways. I don't call people because they are qualified. I qualify those I call. You see it's not about her and her abilities. It's all about me. It's my touch that makes the difference. Do you remember the story about the violin that was being auctioned for sale? No one wanted to offer even a dollar for it. It was so beat up. But when the master violinist came and took it in his hands and played, then the bidding started at a million dollars. When I put my hands on a life, no matter how beat up it might be, the value increases to a point of being priceless. Like when the little boy gave me his lunch of five loaves of bread and two fish and I used it to feed thousands, I can take the little she has to offer and my touch will multiply it. That's just the way I operate. I'm God."

GOD DOES USE THE UNLIKELY

God uses ordinary people. Ultimately, it is not about the person he uses, it's about him. God does not choose those who the world would choose. He makes this clear in 1 Corinthians 1:

> The foolishness of God is wiser than men, and the weakness of God is stronger than men.
>
> For you see your calling, brethren, that not many wise according to the flesh, not many mighty, not many noble, are called. But God has chosen the foolish things of the world to put to shame the wise, and God has chosen the weak things of the world to put to shame the things which are mighty; and the base things of the world and the things which are despised God has chosen, and the things which are not, to bring to nothing the things that are, that no flesh should glory in His presence. (1 Corinthians 1:25-29)

God has chosen me. God has chosen other women. God has chosen other African Americans. God has chosen African American women. African American women have been rejected and despised, but God has chosen us.

As an African American woman, when God spoke to me that he wanted to use me, I felt unqualified. I have had a big-time struggle with fear. In fact, I argued with God that he could not possibly want to use me. In my tradition, to do what he was calling me to do was unusual; it seemed that God usually used men and most often men who were not of my ethnic background. Now, why would he want to go out of the ordinary and use me? But it was not about me. It was about God.

"But, Lord, I don't have a Bible school education or a seminary degree."

"And?"

"Isn't that a criterion?"

"Did my Son have one?"

"No, but he had a close relationship with you."

"And your point was?"

"Well, okay. But Jesus, Paul, Peter and all of them were men."

"How about Mary, the one who brought him onto the earth? Wasn't she a woman?"

"Yeah, but what about my husband?"

"Consider Joseph."

"Okay, Lord, but I don't have national exposure through a TV or radio program. I heard those things are essential to be successful in ministry. I don't have a church with people and the finances to help me accomplish this big vision you have for me. Not many people know me. I have nothing, but . . . well, never mind. I don't want to hurt your feelings."

"I can finish that thought. You have nothing, but me."

"Yeah. It's not that you're not enough. It's just that, you know, people like the flashy, flamboyant, charismatic, articulate type. That's just not me."

"But you have me."

"Yeah, I know. But I don't have money. My personality is too laid back. I don't do well marketing myself."

"But you have me."

"Yeah, I heard you. But the message you've given me is not too popular either. Could I have one of those feel-good ones that will make people flock to me? I mean, that's the least you could do if you want me to serve you in this way."

"You have me."

Though I put up all kinds of arguments about why I thought he must be mistaken, God answered all of my objections. To be doing what I do today—challenging well-established mindsets—is certainly not what I wanted to do, and it is not the best way to win friends and influence people. But then again, it is not about me. My life is not my own, I have been bought with a price. As God's servant, I no longer get a chance to choose what is convenient; he makes the choices.

I submit that many women struggle within themselves about God's ability to use them. Many African American women do not feel qualified to be used of God as the tools he would use to bring defeat to the enemy. Many of us have been conditioned to think we would be the last ones God would choose. Many African American women are fearful. Many of us struggle with esteem issues. We do not see ourselves as mighty women of valor. We see ourselves as the least of the household of God.

I recently met an extremely gifted African American woman. My oldest son heard her speak. He told her, "You need to meet my mom." And he set out to make sure we met each other. I met her and found out how talented she is. She does workshops for teens on self-esteem. She has incredible gifts. She writes, draws, paints and she is a powerful speaker. She has a well-placed job. She has a family that loves her. Yet she admits she has struggled with esteem for a variety of reasons. Unbelievable! You would think that someone that "blessed" and gifted would not have those challenges. But I do understand. In spite of how God has used my writing and speaking to bless others, I have struggled and sometimes still struggle with feelings of low self-esteem.

It really does not matter how talented we might be, many of us still have esteem issues just as Gideon had. It has appeared that we are the least of all the families in Israel. Now, I'm not talking about outwardly. African American women can have it going on from an outward viewpoint. But inwardly, we face many doubts, fears and insecurities. But God will take African American women who struggle with fear and insecurities, and he will use them in mighty ways to bring defeat to the enemy of God. We may be insignificant in our own eyes, but with God, we are mighty.

Our perspective of ourselves has been shaped by what others think of us, not by what God thinks of us. When God begins to speak to us and call us the way he sees us—powerful, chosen vessels—like Gideon, we will propose arguments, trying to resist the call of God on our lives.

Some of us will get on a ship and go in the opposite direction, much like the prophet Jonah, who in running from God's call ended up in the belly of a big fish (Jonah 1—4).

Not only does God have to convince us that he is the one who asks us to join with him, but he also has to convince us of our true identity. God draws close to us. His presence changes the way we think of ourselves. We begin to see ourselves through his eyes. We have to stop thinking of ourselves the way we have always thought of ourselves. It is imperative that we do not even pay attention to how others see us.

Our biggest enemy is our own thoughts about ourselves. Who are we to say God cannot use us? It's like a slap in God's face. He has already made it clear to us that it's not about us. The choice was his. The power comes from him. The strategy comes from him. The credit also belongs to him. We struggle with unbelief and fear because we make our limitations greater than the bigness of God. Instead of exalting the Lord above our weaknesses and fears, we magnify our natural abilities over I AM, the one who brought the worlds into existence by his spoken word.

All he needs to do is speak life to us, which he did through the sacrifice of his Son, and wants to continue to do as he draws close to us and draws us close to himself.

THERE IS A GOD

We really don't know the ways of God. God is God and he's God all by himself. God heals wounds. God is able to transform us (yes, even African American women with issues) in such a way that he can use us to change the world. And you and everybody else will know it wasn't about you or me. It's about a big God!

After God has worked on us, in us, around us and through us, people will not see us, they'll see God. When they look at me, they will remember what I used to be. But they won't see that anymore. They'll see such a reflection of God's glory, they'll be forced to admit, "It's true. God does exist."

I was telling someone the other day about how I love to get in front of a crowd and speak. I can hardly wait until they finish the songs so I can get up there. But if you knew me about twenty years ago, you would not believe I was the same person. There was a time when I hated to get up in front of people. There was a time when I almost quit a job because it required speaking in front of others. But because of the work of God in my life and because of a process of change that I have undergone, I am not the same person.

This change did not come about because of a plan I had put together. I did not listen to tapes on how to overcome the fear of speaking. The power and peace of God is being manifested in my life in such a way that I can only give him the credit. That's a reflection of God's glory in my life.

In fact, a few years ago, my brother Tim came to hear me speak. He had asked me on the phone, "Becky, you get paid for speaking?" He couldn't believe it. He had to come see for himself. He remembered me as the shy girl who was ashamed of her height. Knowing me in the formative years of my life, he remembered the speech difficulties: stuttering, mumbling and other problems that required speech therapy as a child. If my brother had any doubts before, he can now say, "There is a God!

Even today, when people first meet me, they are usually surprised when they hear me speak. I am just not the same person. The hand of God on my life as I get up to speak makes me a different person. In spite of who I am, with all of my strengths and weaknesses, adding God to the equation takes my life to a level that is beyond the natural.

Recently I ran into a lady who I last saw a few years ago. The last time I saw her, she was under a tremendous assault of the enemy with her life reflecting turmoil and confusion. But when I saw her last week, I saw the glory of God manifested in her life. She had completed an advanced degree and was on her way out of state to work in a school for troubled youth. She was a far cry from the lady I had seen a few years ago. That's God.

African American women have been called and chosen to bring glory to God. The good news is that God has already made an investment into our life to glorify himself. It's up to us to find out how we come on up to God's plans and purposes.

WOMEN WALKING IN DIVINE DESTINY

We should be determined to do whatever it takes to find and walk in our purpose. Know that when we walk in our purpose, we will become a barrier to Satan's plans. I want to see women rise to all God has purposed for them so that the enemy of our soul will go down in defeat.

We've got to see things from God's perspective, the spiritual perspective. If we see it just from the natural, we'll never understand what it is that God wants to show us. We'll be hindered from walking in our destiny. We'll always be trying to understand the whys of things. It is impossible to figure God out.

In my first book, *Chosen Vessels: Women of Color, Keys to Change*, I introduced the point that God put enmity between Satan and the woman. I also spoke of the resulting hatred Satan has for women. As punishment for Satan's part in orchestrating the Fall, in Genesis 3:15 we find God threatening the enemy. The Lord God says to the serpent, "I will put enmity between you and the woman, and between your seed and her Seed."

Women are on the same side as God, and we have a common enemy. In fact, *a woman teamed up with God is Satan's biggest nightmare.* Because God chose to use women to bring defeat to his personal enemy, we can be assured that God will do whatever is necessary in our lives to bring us to the place where we are totally God-dependent. God knows what he is doing.

God has an awesome investment in us. He sent his only Son into the world to reverse the damage Satan has done and to empower us to bring an end to Satan's plan. Jesus gave his own life. Romans 8:15 says we have the very life of Christ; the same Spirit who raised Christ from the dead now dwells in us.

God has invested his own power in order for us to be able to execute all he wants us to do. God has also given us his own weapons. As the Word of God tells us in 2 Corinthians 10:

> For the weapons of our warfare are not carnal but mighty in God for pulling down strongholds, casting down arguments and every high thing that exalts itself against the knowledge of God, bringing every thought into captivity to the obedience of Christ, and being ready to punish all disobedience when your obedience is fulfilled. (2 Corinthians 10:4-6)

The weapons of God help us pull down strongholds. There are many wrong thought patterns in our mind that need to be pulled down. And God has given us weapons to be able to pull those things down. God has given grace and strength.

He gave us grace to come boldly to the throne of grace to ask for mercy and help in our time of need (Hebrews 4:16). We have access to the Father whenever we need help; whenever we need wisdom for a situation, we have access to the Father. We can go in his presence and say, "God, I need help." God's Word says his strength is made perfect in our weakness (2 Corinthians 12:9); so when we are weak, when we don't know what to do, we can call on his strength. He's given us his love. God loves us so dearly, he wants us to understand the height, and the breadth and the depth of his love (Ephesians 3:18). God has given us all we need that pertains to life and godliness (2 Peter 1:3). All means everything.

The only reason we're missing it is because we don't know what we have. And the reason we don't know what we have is because we've been listening to too many of Satan's lies.

God has pulled out all the stops to get us to the place of truth and freedom to be all he had originally destined us to be. The difficulty we have with walking in our freedom is based on what we believe. Many of us have believed numerous lies about our value and worth. We have believed lies about God's love for us. In our minds, there are deeply ingrained lies about God's purpose for our lives. We hold on to deceptions about spiritual maturity.

Women need to seek understanding about the ways of God. When we understand his ways, we can move from much of the struggle, frustration and confusion that plagues us on a daily basis. We can move into the peace and rest of God. So let's continue to tear down mental strongholds so that we will be able to stand in our position. And after having done all to the glory of God, let us continue to stand.

Part three

Speaking to the Unseen

11

THE UNSEEN
BEHIND THE SCENE

M y husband and I went to see a play. That evening we saw the actors on the stage. In the program, many people were acknowledged that we never saw. There was a stage manager, a set designer, sound technicians, makeup artists and others. People came quickly on the stage to change the set in between scenes. We saw a play, but there was a lot going on behind the scenes that we, as the audience, never saw.

Somebody was watching over everything. There was a director of the play who knew everything that was going on. It wasn't useful for the audience to see everything. It would have been cumbersome and boring to watch the things going on behind the scenes. And the director's work started long before that night. His involvement may have started two years prior to that night as he selected the play. There was the selection of the actors, the rehearsals, set design. I could go on and on, but you get the picture. For a play, a whole lot goes on behind the scenes.

So, what does that have to do with the understanding that it's not about you? Well, in life, there is action behind the scenes that we don't always see, but we need to know about it. The divine director knows everything. We can trust him to make the right decisions with his knowledge of what is behind the scenes. We can trust that he has been working on this production for a long time.

Yes, he chose us to be a part of the play, and we need to learn our part. However, the set design, the makeup artists, the stage managers are really not our concern. It's good to know that stagehands will come in between the scenes and do their job. We can relax and do what we need to do without having to worry that it'll get done. The director is taking care of all of that.

I suppose it would be ideal to just enjoy the play and not even think about the happenings behind the scene. I guess if I were an actor, it would be less stressful to just do my part and not worry about anything else. But I'm curious. I wouldn't mind a tour of what goes on behind closed doors.

BEHIND THE SCENES

There are times when it is good to have the knowledge of what goes on behind the scenes to really appreciate the things we do see. That's why tours of operations are so popular for school field trips or vacations.

I chaperoned on a school trip once that visited a chocolate factory. We were taken on a tour behind the scenes. We were shown how the chocolate was made. We saw all of the machinery, the molds and the workers. When we finished the tour, we came into a shop area where the chocolate was on display. Having seen the work behind the scenes, we could better appreciate the final product. (Not that I wouldn't have appreciated it before the tour. Trust me, put a few macadamias or walnuts with that chocolate and you have my utmost appreciation. But that's beside the point.)

Just as seeing the behind the scenes operation can sometimes help, likewise, it is okay to know what is going on behind the scenes of life in order to make it through another day. No, we do not need to dwell on the behind the scenes stuff. But one little glimpse might take us a long way.

Once, an assistant of a man of God was very stressed out by the things he could see. He was not having a good day. There was an army surrounding him. According to what he could see, he probably needed to call his attorney to see if his will was up to date. This was probably going to be his last day on this earth.

THE SCENE BEHIND THE UNSEEN

The following account from history shows us a number of truths about unseen forces. I've decided to include it here in a modern version so it'll flow more like a story, a scene from a picture. It is taken from 2 Kings 6:11-23 in the Living Translation.

The king of Syria was puzzled. He called together his officers and demanded, "Which of you is the traitor? Who has been informing the king of Israel about my plans?"

"It's not us, sir," one of the officers replied. "Elisha, the prophet, tells the king of Israel even the words you speak in the privacy of your bedroom!"

"Go and find out where he is, and we'll send troops to seize him," the king exclaimed.

And the report came back, "Elisha is at Dothan."

So one night the king of Syria sent a great army with many chariots and horses to surround the city. When the prophet's servant got up early the next morning and went outside, there were troops, horses and chariots everywhere.

"Alas, my master, what shall we do now?" he cried out to Elisha.

"Don't be afraid!" Elisha told him. "For our army is bigger than theirs!"

Then Elisha prayed, "Lord, open his eyes and let him see!" And the Lord opened the young man's eyes so that he could see horses of fire and chariots of fire everywhere on the mountain!

As the Syrian army advanced on them, Elisha prayed, "Lord, please make them blind." And he did.

Then Elisha went out and told them, "You've come the wrong way! This isn't the right city! Follow me and I will take you to the man you're looking for." And he led them to Samaria!

As soon as they arrived Elisha prayed, "Lord, now open their eyes and let them see." And the Lord did, and they discovered that they were in Samaria, the capital city of Israel!

When the king of Israel saw them, he shouted to Elisha, "Oh, sir, shall I kill them? Shall I kill them?"

"Of course not!" Elisha told him. "Do we kill prisoners of war? Give them food and drink, and send them home again."

So the king made a great feast for them and then sent them home to their king. And after that the Syrian raiders stayed away from the land of Israel.

Isn't that story really cool? I love this picture. Did you catch the unseen behind the scene? Elisha's servant was afraid of what he saw in the natural. He could see with his eyes that the armies surrounding them were insurmountable. But Elisha, who God allowed to see behind the scene, was not afraid. He was not moved by what the enemy came up with. He knew God had his back. But it's hard to be unconcerned when the person who is working with you is throwing a fit, so Elisha asked God to open the eyes of his servant so he could see what Elisha already knew was there.

OUR EYES NEED TO BE OPENED

African American Christian women, there is a lot unseen behind the seen scene. There is the natural world in which we live. We know about this world through our five physical senses. The things we touch, see, hear, smell and taste are real. But just as real is the world of the unseen. In it, God exists. He is invisible to our five senses. Also in this world are spiritual beings called angels. This was the host that Elisha's servant was enabled to see when God opened his eyes. These angels are on God's side and respond to his commands.

I'm not sure if Elisha could see into the spiritual realm at will. I suspect he was just close enough to God that he knew what was in the invisible world. We have that same privilege as we draw close to God and stay close to him. We'll become more and more comfortable with not having to see everything. We'll just know that there is much in the unseen realm. Without having to see it, we can be assured God has an army working on our behalf. That's what walking by faith is all about.

Many times, we are like Elisha's servant. When we don't know about the scene behind the unseen, we tend to worry and fret. In the late eighties when we lived in Chicago, my husband was unemployed. He had worked for a contract company. When his temporary assignment was over, he did not immediately have another position. He had done contract work for a while and decided he would look for a permanent position. He had been looking, but nothing came through right away.

I was working part time and was able to increase my hours during this period, but it still was not enough to cover our monthly budget. I began to worry that we might not have enough to pay all of our bills. I did not think about the scene behind the unseen. I concentrated on what my eyes could see. My eyes only saw bills beginning to pile up and the mortgage note coming due.

I intellectually knew according to Philippians 4:6 that I should not worry about anything. I knew the Word of God told us to be anxious for nothing. Yet, I worried. I did not have the peace of God. Peace and worry cannot coexist. If our spiritual eyes could be open at all times to see what God has in store, we would stop wasting so much time worrying and being anxious.

Since we live in natural bodies and most of us will not see into the spiritual realm at all times, what is the alternative? The alternative is to keep our eyes on God. He promises us perfect peace as our eyes are stayed on him (Isaiah 23:6). We may not always see what God sees, but we can be assured that, as we look to God rather than looking at our circumstances, we can be at peace.

God's provisions, resources and help are not always visible in the natural realm. God himself is invisible. But he manifests himself and that which he has to offer in the natural realm as needed. We only need to know him and know that what he has available in the invisible realm is available to us as we trust him. All we need is God.

During that period, God was faithful. Our mortgage company contacted us and told us we had excess in our account and did not have to send in a payment that month. Hallelujah! I wasted a lot of time trying to figure out how we were going to pay the mortgage. God had it all worked out way ahead of time. It was no coincidence that they happened to let us know of the overpayment that month. It was not a chance happening that the amount was enough to cover a whole month's payment.

Many of us can tell of how trust in God led to his provision. In Nashville, a dear sister in the Lord told me how God provided for her son when he was involved in a very serious car accident years ago. He was at death's door, in intensive care for two months.

He had just started a new job and, as far as they were concerned, there was no need to worry about adequate medical coverage. However, when he ended up in the hospital, they soon discovered that his insurance was not in effect at the time of the accident.

They were stuck with thousands of dollars in medical bills. Even though her son was twenty-one and the mother still was told she was not legally responsible for the bills, this mother discussed with the hospital a method of slowly paying off the bills.

But God had other plans. She was told about a program that might be able to help. She filled out the appropriate papers and the whole hospital bill was paid, close to $30,000. God had resources available that she knew nothing about. But he made sure she found out about them.

She still had physician's bills to pay. These were in addition to the hospital bills. Of course, she was unable to pay those either. One day she received a letter that said she had to show up in court. It appeared she was being sued over the payment owed to the doctors. Not knowing what to do, she discussed her situation with one of her coworkers. He put her in touch with his son who was an attorney. The son referred her to another attorney who was a friend of his.

She followed the advice of the attorney, and it turned out that this bill ended up being written off without her having to pay. She never heard from the doctors again. The attorney knew that, because her son had been told he would never be able to work again, the doctors would just write the loss off. But the doctors had to prove they had attempted to collect the money before they could do that—that was the reason she was summoned to court.

In all, God provided for close to $40,000 worth of bills. When God tells us not to worry, it's because he has things we know not of. He has unseen provisions behind the scene.

GOD WILL MAKE A WAY

God has a variety of ways of working behind the scene to bring the unseen into the seen. This dear lady could have worried about going out to get an extra $40,000. She could have concentrated her energies on borrowing, taking out a loan, getting a second mortgage on her house or working several jobs for many years. Her focus would have been too narrow.

Many times, we see a need and only think of what is needed to meet the need. We concentrate on getting that provision. But we need to let go of our thoughts of how the need will be met. What this woman really needed was to be at zero debt. Yes, she needed $40,000 to get there, but she did not necessarily need to be the one who came up with the

$40,000. She didn't need to focus all of her attention and prayers on getting the $40,000 into her hands and taking it to the hospital to pay off the debt.

God gave her zero debt by having another program pay $30,000 and allowing the $10,000 to be canceled. I think we often miss God because we concentrate on the wrong things.

Let's suppose Chosen Vessels Ministries, a ministry to develop women who minister to other women, has in its budget a need for $1,000 for office supplies and furniture, $20,000 for office staff, and $2,000 for professional services such as bookkeeping, legal assistance, editing and so on. I could concentrate on where is $23,000 going to come from, or I could just concentrate on the end result: staffing needs, office furniture and supplies, and professional services.

By doing the latter I can allow God to bring provisions in from behind the scenes into the seen. Yes, he could allow me to receive a grant of $23,000 that would pay for all that I needed. Or he could have a generous donor give $3,000 and have two retired people come to volunteer and meet all of the staffing needs. Maybe I do not get any money at all, but he might meet these needs through volunteers, an offer from an office supply store to come in and pick up all the office supplies I need free of charge, and donations from a furniture store that is going out of business.

God himself is the supplier of all of our needs (Philippians 4:19). When we step out of the way, the supplier can bring the supplies to us from behind the scenes.

When the disciples needed food to feed the thousands, they could have had a committee to discuss how they were going to raise the money needed to hire a catering service to feed so many people or how they were going to be able to bring all of those sandwiches from the local Subway. Again, they would have been wasting their time. The need was food for 5,000 people, not catering or transportation. God met the need by multiplying a little boy's lunch.

The widow in 2 Kings 4 had a need to pay off debt. God met the need by taking what was in her hand and multiplying it to fill the vessels she had available so that she could sell it to meet the need. We have to get a revelation of God's greatness. God is so marvelous that if we add him to anything, whether good or bad, we will get good. Add him to a mess and you'll get all things, whether good or bad, working together for good. Add him to a lack and you'll have a provision if you keep your mind open to creative ways and your eyes open to look in unusual places.

Lord, Can't You Show Me?

I would not have any trouble with worry if I could only know about the unseen resources. Even if God chose not to show them to me, I just want him to tell me what they are, where they are and that he will provide them in due time.

In reality, he has already told us about them. In his Word, he has given us precious promises of his provisions (Philippians 4:19). No, we may not know all of the details, but we don't have to know that. We just need to know that he's got it covered and he is faithful.

Is it possible to view the difficult events in life as God's intended means to force us to see beyond the veil into another realm? Could it be when we are outnumbered by our enemies that God wanted all along for us to get so desperate that we'd cry out to him and so he could show us the unseen army that is already on our side?

Tight places, tight circumstances should lead us to the discovery that it's not about us or even up to us to defend ourselves. We should come away from a situation in which we experience need with a greater revelation of the greatness of God. Big battles should demonstrate just how much bigger our God is. Impossible situations show us that with God nothing is impossible. Vast needs show us the immeasurable nature of our God.

A friend of mine, Joy Gaddis, who God uses to minister to many through speaking, was telling me how someone came up to her after she had ministered and asked for prayer so that she too could have the same "anointing" to do great things for God. My friend looked at her and said, "Are you ready for some great trouble?" We don't understand that the capacity to be used of God is developed through situations that knock the very wind out of our sails so that God himself ends up being the wind and the sails that move us.

God will not always tell us everything about what he has in store for us. God reserves the right to keep some things to himself. God has given us enough of what his intentions are for us in his Word. He has already told us that he will supply all of our needs according to his riches in glory by Christ Jesus (Philippians 4:19). There has to be an element of faith.

Let's face it: we want to know everything so that we will no longer need faith. Actually, we want it so we no longer need God. Now I know it would be difficult for us to admit to this, but think about it. If you knew everything about everything, would you still need God? No. In fact, God is the only one who knows everything about everything. If we want that position, then we are saying we want to be God.

God is looking for co-laborers like Elisha who know him in a close relationship. God does not need co-gods. As co-laborers, together we can spoil the enemy's plan against our families and communities. God has a lot of things in store for us that we cannot see. They are the unseen scene. Though we can't always see them, they are just as real as the host of armed forces God let Elisha's servant see in a moment in time.

Can you trust God even when you don't know the unseen behind the scene? Maybe God will not open your spiritual eyes to see behind the scene, but he has given you his Word that describes the provisions he has prepared for us. We can see the spiritual unseen behind the seen when we draw closer to God in fellowship and in his Word.

Just as God had an invisible force standing behind the scene ready to go into battle at his bidding for Elisha and his servant, those forces are still ready today to do God's bidding for all of God's purposes under the sun.

12

SATAN'S WAYS

Wₑ have established the existence of the unseen behind the seen. We made the point that much more takes place than what we see on a daily basis. While our major focus is on what takes place in the physical realm, God has a point or points to make to the unseen realm. God may speak to the unseen evil forces through our lives. Among the unseen are forces called "principalities and powers in the heavenly places" (Ephesians 3:10). In the following passage, Paul tells us that God makes known his wisdom to principalities and powers by using his church.

> To the intent that now the manifold wisdom of God might be made known by the church to the principalities and powers in the heavenly places, according to the eternal purpose which He accomplished in Christ Jesus our Lord, in whom we have boldness and access with confidence through faith in him. (Ephesians 3:10-12)

THE EVIL UNSEEN SOURCE

Satan is an evil unseen force. He lives in heavenly places. Let's take a look at Satan, the force of evil in the unseen world. We may be able to get a glimpse of the points God wants to make and also see why. A passage of Scripture in Isaiah 14 speaks of his downfall.

> How you are fallen from heaven,
> O Lucifer, son of the morning!
> How you are cut down to the ground,
> You who weakened the nations!
> For you have said in your heart:

"I will ascend into heaven,
I will exalt my throne above the stars of God;
I will also sit on the mount of the congregation
On the farthest sides of the north;
I will ascend above the heights of the clouds,
I will be like the Most High." (Isaiah 14:12-14)

What God wants to accomplish through his people, particularly women, is something that is going to counteract the very things that Satan originally brought into the universe. You can see what that is in this passage. This passage contains a series of "I will" statements: "I will ascend into heaven." "I will exalt my throne above the stars of God." "I will also sit on the mount of the congregation." "I will ascend above the heights of the clouds." "I will be like the Most High."

Whenever I ask audiences to tell me in one word what these "I will" statements indicate, the answer usually given is pride. Of course, that is what I'm looking for. Satan brought pride into the universe. Pride came into all of us when Adam and Eve took of the tree of the knowledge of good and evil. We were born with pride. We got it from Satan who is the father of everyone until they are born again.

In the passage of Scripture in Isaiah, we see Satan as the epitome of pride. Pride wants to be like God. Pride wants to be above God. Pride desires to be able to do without God. Pride wants to be in the same arena in which God resides.

Essentially, pride is opposite of the position of rest. When we rest in God, we cease from our own anxious activity. Rest is a place of trust in the ability of God to be in charge. Rest is a place of peace that defies understanding. Rest is being comfortable without having to know or understand the hows, whens, wheres, whats and whys of a matter.

Pride is what we are and do when we try to operate as co-gods. It's when we try to give God our counsel. It's when we trip out when something unexpected happens. We're upset because God did not seek our advice or because he did not warn us ahead of time. Pride is when we just have to know something concrete before we can make a move. We cannot just take God's Word on it. Faith, the substance of things hoped for, is just too vague for us.

We know that God hates pride (Proverbs 6:16). Pride is what Satan has brought onto the earth. Satan epitomizes pride. All of us were poisoned with pride from Satan.

ARE YOU INVITING THE ENEMY INTO YOUR LIFE?

"I'm going to do what I want to do when I want to, and nobody is going to stop me." I . . . I . . . I . . . Much of our self-centered attitude is one of pride and rebellion, the principles of Satan. Walking in Satan's ways will only invite Satan into our lives to work havoc by killing, stealing and destroying. If we want to evict the devil from our lives, homes, churches and communities, we need to practice humility. This will cleanse us and take out the stain of rebelliousness.

This is a very important point, one that we need to take under serious consideration. Much of the activity of the enemy in our lives, our families and our communities is there because we have given him an invitation by having defiant attitudes to come in and do his damage. Murmuring and complaining is an indication of that attitude. God has given us many examples in his Word of the dangers of murmuring and complaining (1 Corinthians 10:10).

Satan's way of strife is opposite of God's way, the way of peace. In order to get out of harm's way, we need to operate out of peace, not strife. When there's strife, when there's self-seeking, when there's an insistence on always having our way, we're opening the door for the demonic. Satan's calling card is I . . . I . . . I . . . Satan is totally self-centered and self-focused. The opposite of self-seeking is yielding. Yielding to another is difficult. But it's the way of God. It's the wisdom that comes from above. And we see in James 3:

> Who is wise and understanding among you? Let him show by good conduct that his works are done in the meekness of wisdom. But if you have bitter envy and self-seeking in your hearts, do not boast and lie against the truth. This wisdom does not descend from above, but is earthly, sensual, demonic. For where envy and self-seeking exist, confusion and every evil thing are there. But the wisdom that is from above is first pure, then peaceable, gentle, willing to yield, full of mercy and good fruits,

without partiality and without hypocrisy. Now the fruit of righteousness is sown in peace by those who make peace. (James
3:13-18)

I believe the way the enemy gets the most mileage out of pride in the
spiritual warfare against our lives is how he uses our minds to accuse
others. He is the accuser of the brethren (Revelation 12:10). Satan will
plant thoughts in our mind concerning another person. We will think
those thoughts are our own. We will accept them, believe them and act
on them. As a result, we will have strife, tension or some kind of es-
trangement from that person. It may be minor or it may be very major,
but the end result is, we are divided.

This is very unfortunate because the power of God against the enemy works best as we are united. Knowing that, I believe Satan's biggest use of pride is to keep people apart. We are in pride when we
accept the accuser of the brethren's verdict about another person.
Who are we to judge another? Even if that which the other person is
being accused of is true, could not the purpose of our knowing about
this truth be to pray for the person? Perhaps, we should get the log out
of our own eye first.

Love covers a multitude of sins. We seriously err when we accept the
accusations against another in our own mind as truth. We are not God.
We do not have the right to pass judgment on another person. The
Word of God tells us that spiritual warfare is casting down imaginations
and every high thing that exalts itself against the knowledge of God
(2 Corinthians 10:4).

We need to use the weapons of our warfare given to us by God to
refuse accusations against others. We need to think on things that are
good, virtuous, praiseworthy (Philippians 4:8).

Our greatest battle is in our mind. That's why it is so important to re-
new our mind. We need to begin to think God's thoughts in his way instead of our own thoughts. We wouldn't receive most of the accusations
about another person if we were not so self-focused. When we think it
is about us, we readily accept the lies from the enemy about another
person.

John Eldredge, the author of *Wild at Heart*, tells of his thoughts of accusation against his wife when she suggested an alternative route to get to their son's soccer game when they were stuck in traffic. He says he was ready for a separation about twenty seconds after he allowed a barrage of thoughts to come to his mind, such as, "Doesn't she think I know how to get there?"

John asks the question, "Has it ever crossed your mind that not every thought that crosses your mind comes from you?" He goes on to say, "What I experienced in the midst of traffic that day happens all the time in marriages, in ministries, in any relationship. We are being lied to all the time. Yet we never stop to say, 'Wait a minute . . . who else is speaking here? Where are those ideas coming from? Where are those *feelings* coming from?'"

EVICTING THE ENEMY

In order to counteract the pride Satan brought onto the earth, God uses humility. Now if God said that he is going to use women to defeat Satan, then one of those things he is trying to do through women is to bring them to a walk in humility. God even goes further to say that he will be near the humble. God resists the proud but has promised to give grace to the humble (James 4:6).

So obviously the most important thing God has to do in our lives is to ensure our walk is in humility, not pride. As long as we're in pride then we're on the wrong side. I don't think we want to be on Satan's side when we're striving for a closer walk with God. If we're in pride, we're basically using Satan's principles.

We can close the door on the devil when he first tries to get in. We have a choice, we have a choice to die to the self-seeking, the I . . . I . . . I . . . I want it this way, I want it that way. We have a choice to submit our personal desires to the will of the Father. We have a choice to choose weakness instead of our own strength. As African American women, we have the choice to walk in humility instead of pride. We have a choice to surrender our ability to understand and control things into the hands of a good God who may not explain anything to us and may only say, "Trust me."

We have a choice to continue to do it the enemy's way and continue to suffer the consequences of inviting him into our lives, or we can send him running by drawing near to God and doing things God's way. Yes, we can send the devil packing. We can close the door on the devil, and we can learn to live in such a way that he won't find an entrance back in.

Refusing pride after we have entertained accusations against another person in our mind will mean that we admit that we don't know if those thoughts are true or not. We give the person the benefit of the doubt. To humble ourselves when we are thinking negative thoughts about another person will mean that we refuse to dwell on the evil about the person. Even if we have all kinds of proof about the evil, we still give the person mercy. God calls us to be merciful as he is merciful (Luke 6:36).

It is much easier to act in pride, in Satan's ways, when we think about others instead of humbling ourselves. But if we want the enemy out of the lives of our family members and our larger community, we first have to evict him and prevent his constant use of our minds as the dumping grounds for his thoughts.

It is humbling to admit that we really don't know why a person did what they did and just leave it alone. We may know what they did was wrong, but it is wrong for us to judge their motives. It is very hard to just let things go. Pride puts us in God's shoes. Not only do we know what they did, we're sure of the reason why they did it, and we can tell everyone how long they thought about doing it and when they are likely to do it again. I don't think so. Only God knows all of that.

GETTING THE PRIDE OUT

I want the pride out of my life. But I want God to take it out quickly. However, I have found that as I walk through a process, God has been faithful to take the pride out. In the processing, I have cried, wrestled with God, questioned God, fasted and prayed. I sought counsel, got depressed and almost gave up. I did everything I could think of. I'm not sure if any of what I did accomplished anything, but in the process of getting in God's face, God changed me.

Now I'm different. I can't explain what brought about the change. It could have been that in wrestling with God, like Jacob, I was left with a limp (Genesis 32:24-31). Maybe it was the tears that changed me. Maybe the waiting and waiting was allowing the Holy Spirit to marinate my life. I'm not sure. But in the process, I've been changed. When it was all over, I found out it was not about me getting what I wanted when I wanted it, but it was about God's purposes and plans all along.

After you go through the process, you're dependent on God and your words are backed with power. God stands behind what you say. That's what God is after: a powerful army of women who're following his every direction. God says, "Go this way." "Turn to the right." God says, "Turn to the left." Because we've learned how to obey in the process, our will is no longer our own will. We've gone to Gethsemane. We have cried, we have fought and we have come to a place of accepting God's ways and God's thoughts even when it does not make sense to us. We are women who say, "I'm going to do it God's way."

Yes, you've been through. However, not only have you come through but you've been changed in the process. You can sing, "A change has come over me." The pride has been taken out.

A Case Study

Joseph was changed in the process. When we first see Joseph in Genesis 37, he was cocky. In telling his brothers about his dream, he probably was rubbing it in. But you see something entirely different in Genesis 41. What happened between chapters 37 and 41? Joseph had been thrown in the pit, sold into slavery, betrayed and put in prison. He had gone through a process. He was not so cocky now. In fact, he appears quite humble.

It became apparent to him that he couldn't do anything without God. It was very apparent he was not in control of what happened and when things happened. God had used him to interpret dreams, but he knew he couldn't even do that if God didn't help him. During the times of disappointment and sorrow in his life, he had drawn close to God.

Finally, Pharaoh has a dream and needs interpretation. He was told about Joseph in Genesis 41.

> Then Pharaoh sent and called Joseph, and they brought him quickly out of the dungeon; and he shaved, changed his clothing, and came to Pharaoh. And Pharaoh said to Joseph, "I have had a dream, and there is no one who can interpret it. But I have heard

it said of you that you can understand a dream, to interpret it."
(Genesis 41:14-15)

Dreams had first revealed the pride in Joseph. Now when he had a
chance to really get proud over dreams, he didn't. Though he still might
not have known the full impact of why God chose him, he was no
longer tripping over what God gave him. By that time, Joseph had humility. All the pride that was in him back when he first got the dreams
about his brothers bowing down to him was gone. Joseph tells Pharaoh,
"I cannot do it, but God will give Pharaoh the answer he desires."

In the beginning, Joseph thought it was about him. Like Joseph, by
the time you wait and wait and wait and wait, and God still doesn't
come through when you think he should come through, you're puri-
fied, washed of the junk that made you the center of the universe.
You've come to the conclusion God's going to do it in his own good
time, and you had better just learn to be patient. You realize that it's not
your timing, it's God's.

Joseph was speaking from the wisdom of God. He was speaking
from his relationship with God. He was hearing from God as he was
talking. He had learned to cultivate that relationship. It says in verse
37 that the plan seemed good to Pharaoh and to all his officials. So
Pharaoh asked them, "Can we find anyone like this man? One in
whom is the Spirit of God?"

> So the advice was good in the eyes of Pharaoh and in the eyes of
> all his servants. And Pharaoh said to his servants, "Can we find
> such a one as this, a man in whom is the Spirit of God?" Then
> Pharaoh said to Joseph, "Inasmuch as God has shown you all this,
> there is no one as discerning and wise as you. You shall be over my
> house, and all my people shall be ruled according to your word;
> only in regard to the throne will I be greater than you." And Phar-
> aoh said to Joseph, "See, I have set you over all the land of Egypt."
> Then Pharaoh took his signet ring off his hand and put it on Jo-
> seph's hand; and he clothed him in garments of fine linen and put
> a gold chain around his neck. And he had him ride in the second
> chariot which he had; and they cried out before him, "Bow the
> knee!" So he set him over all the land of Egypt. (Genesis 41:37-43)

GOD REVEALS HIMSELF TO US

We learn to walk in the Spirit as a result of trials, tribulations, betrayals and disappointments. We learn to do things God's way — we pray for our enemies. We learn to give up bitterness. We learn to forgive. After the process, the people around you see your walk in the Spirit. They recognize the Spirit of God in you and on you.

You have learned it's not about you and have come to know God better. The following poem, "My Name Is Joseph," from A *Diary of Joseph* is a powerful portrayal of these points.

Greetings, my brothers
My name is Joseph.
It means "Increaser."
I didn't understand that when you put me in the pit.
I didn't know it in Potiphar's house.
I started to learn it in prison.
But now I *know*.
I know that you meant it for evil, but God meant it for good.
I understand now.

It's not about me.
It's not about my dreams, though I appreciate them.
It's about the One who gave me the interpretation.
It's not about my visions.
It's about the One who gave me sight.

I just had to know it for myself.
So I thank God for you, dear brothers.
My father taught me, and I never forgot, I just had to learn
    with my heart.
I am poured out into his hands;
He is able to hold my life.

In Genesis 50:20, Joseph says to his brothers, "But as for you, you meant evil against me; but God meant it for good, in order to bring it about as it is this day, to save many people alive." So in all the processing, he came to the conclusion that even though his brothers were used to inflict evil on him, it still turned out for good. With pride gone, he could now look at people through the eyes of God. Joseph had learned to refuse the accusations of the enemy concerning his brothers.

So we, too, can say, "Even if this person hurts me, God can work it out for good. All that happened to me, Satan you intended it for evil, but God intended it for good." And when you can come to that point—where you can kiss the hand that hurts you, where you can say, "You might have intended this for evil, but God intended it for good"—the process has done its work. The pride has been taken out. Your thought processes are changed. You now think like God, overcoming evil with good. You don't receive accusations about others in your mind because you realize that even if they happen to be pawns in the enemy's hand, God still has the ability to make it all work together for good.

God processes us when he shows us his ways instead of his acts. In the process, we are transformed into the image of his dear Son. In the process, we mature. We draw nigh to God and actually become more like God. That is more precious to God than our having comfortable lives of ease with no problems, no challenges, nothing to cause us to call out to God.

God is looking for people who have been through the process, people who have learned to depend on him. God looks for the treasure in earthen vessels. As we commit to desire that treasure more than we want anything else, we can have a God-perspective on the circumstances of life. When we are willing to sell everything we have to buy the field of great price, we will have finally realized the true value of the ways of God versus his acts.

Not only will God get the pride out of us through a process of taking us through things we cannot understand or things that are difficult, he offers us a way we can purposely humble ourselves.

13

JOB, I BRAGGED ON YOU

Women often ask, "Why do we go through so much pain?" It is necessary to see the things we go through in the context of God's integrity. Not only do we need to see God's spiritual armies, we need to understand that there are often spiritual purposes behind what we go through. We often ask the wrong questions. When things happen to us, we often wonder, "Why me?" But "why me?" is the wrong question. I heard someone say, "Why not you?" That's something to ponder.

In this chapter, we will look at a person who entrusted himself into the hands of God and probably endured some of the worst suffering any one person could endure. We will also consider how understanding the purposes of God and what went on behind closed doors was an integral part of what took place. Perhaps we, too, can gain a clearer perspective about our life with God and the things that happen to us. Perhaps we, too, will come to the conclusion that it really isn't about us.

When Job suffered his losses, he was not aware of what had transpired behind the scenes between God and the enemy of God. I'm sure he could not figure out why he had to go through so much unnecessary suffering. Hopefully, by the time you finish this chapter, we'll destroy the myth that we sometimes go through more than necessary. It's only more than we can handle if we forget that it is not about us.

WHAT ARE YOU SAYING TO UNSEEN ENTITIES?
It really isn't about us humans. It's about principalities and powers of a different substance. Human beings are just players who determine who

will win this battle on an entirely higher plane. We saw there were unseen resources and beings behind the scene. There are also entities who have meetings, discussions, bets—all behind the scene.

"Therefore we also, since we are surrounded by so great a cloud of witnesses, let us lay aside every weight, and the sin which so easily ensnares us, and let us run with endurance the race that is set before us" (Hebrews 12:1). Because of the unseen entities watching us, we are instructed regarding how to run our race. It appears that the way we run our race is part of what is being watched.

Down here in the physical, we watch games. In the spiritual world, humans are watched. The spiritual realm is watching the physical. I personally believe the ones who have gone before us, who are up in heaven, also have the opportunity to watch us. I picture them cheering us on. That's just what I imagine.

Though I don't have any proof, I believe the cloud of witnesses are the people of God in heaven. There is no question or doubt in my mind that Jesus is intimately concerned about what goes on down here, what happens to his children. Through his sacrifice on the cross, he has done all he needs to do to provide us with what we need for total victory. He has given us everything we need for life and godliness (2 Peter 1:3). He even now lives to pray for us (Hebrews 7:25).

The fact of the matter is, we're in the game. It's a race and it's a fight. Both pictures are given in Scripture. Besides God, spiritual entities, angels and demons are definitely a part of that cloud that surrounds us and watches us. What we do down here is being observed. Our responses to things that happen are very important. Our behavior determines how we do in the race. There is a winner. Paul talks about this race in other passages. We should strive to win. In the passage below, we see a reference to a race as well as a fight.

> Do you not know that those who run in a race all run, but one receives the prize? Run in such a way that you may obtain it. And everyone who competes for the prize is temperate in all things. Now they do it to obtain a perishable crown, but we for an imperishable crown. Therefore I run thus: not with uncertainty. Thus I fight: not as one who beats the air. But I discipline my body and

bring it into subjection, lest, when I have preached to others, I myself should become disqualified. (1 Corinthians 9:24-27)

We note here there are also two pictures of fighting; one is a wrestling match, the other is a war.

I have fought the good fight, I have finished the race, I have kept the faith. (2 Timothy 4:7)

Finally, my brethren, be strong in the Lord and in the power of His might. Put on the whole armor of God, that you may be able to stand against the wiles of the devil. For we do not wrestle against flesh and blood, but against principalities, against powers, against the rulers of the darkness of this age, against spiritual hosts of wickedness in the heavenly places. Therefore take up the whole armor of God, that you may be able to withstand in the evil day, and having done all, to stand. Stand therefore, having girded your waist with truth, having put on the breastplate of righteousness, and having shod your feet with the preparation of the gospel of peace; above all, taking the shield of faith with which you will be able to quench all the fiery darts of the wicked one. And take the helmet of salvation, and the sword of the Spirit, which is the word of God. (Ephesians 6:10-17)

You therefore must endure hardship as a good soldier of Jesus Christ. No one engaged in warfare entangles himself with the affairs of this life, that he may please him who enlisted him as a soldier. And also if anyone competes in athletics, he is not crowned unless he competes according to the rules. (2 Timothy 2:3-5)

Our actions and attitudes have a direct impact on the unseen realm. We have the opportunity to speak volumes to the unseen world. The question is, What are you saying to unseen entities? How's your fight? How's your race?

As stated earlier, when things happen to us, we often ask, "Why me?" As we grow to realize it is not about us, the self-focused questions will not be necessary. The questions will take a different twist.

- "Could God be using this in the battle with Satan?"

- "What is God up to?"
- "What's the big picture here?"
- "God, what do you need me to do to make you look good?"
- "Lord, what are you going to show me about yourself?"

THE CASE OF JOB

Recently, I heard someone say that the angels who are around the throne in heaven are still discovering facets of God they had not seen before. Job, a man who went through a lot of suffering, also received a higher view of God as a result of God entering into his pain. Again, when we add God to anything, he has the ability to transform that thing into something positive.

You have suffered some. I have suffered some. But probably your sufferings and mine together, along with ten others, would not add up to what Job suffered. Let's say you are going through some very rough times. You do not understand why things are happening the way they are. This may not be your current experience, but I think most of us can identify. It's happened at one time or another. Let's say you spent some time fasting and praying, asking God to show you what in the world is going on in your life. What if God answered, "It is not about you. There are some things that are going on behind the scene. I cannot even tell you about it all right now. You've just got to trust me"? Essentially, that was God's answer to Job's questions about why he had to go through so much.

Let's take a look at Job in the book named after him. According to the first chapter of the book, Job lived in the land of Uz. He was blameless and upright, a man who feared God and had nothing to do with evil. He had seven sons and three daughters. He was very rich, owning lots of sheep, camels, oxen and donkeys. He was esteemed as a great man.

> Now there was a day when the sons of God came to present themselves before the LORD, and Satan also came among them. And the LORD said to Satan, "From where do you come?" So Satan answered the LORD and said, "From going to and fro on the earth, and from walking back and forth on it." Then the LORD said to Satan, "Have you considered My servant Job, that there is none like

him on the earth, a blameless and upright man, one who fears God and shuns evil?" So Satan answered the LORD and said, "Does Job fear God for nothing? Have You not made a hedge around him, around his household, and around all that he has on every side? You have blessed the work of his hands, and his possessions have increased in the land. But now, stretch out Your hand and touch all that he has, and he will surely curse You to Your face!" And the LORD said to Satan, "Behold, all that he has is in your power; only do not lay a hand on his person." So Satan went out from the presence of the LORD. (Job 1:6-12)

Here we see one of those meetings that take place in the unseen world. At this particular meeting, Satan presents himself before the Lord. The Lord asks him where he came from, and Satan told him that he had been going back and forth on the earth.

I have never seen Satan walking on this earth. I guess he doesn't walk around where I've been. Well, that's not true. Even if he walks around the places you happen to be, you will not see him. But you can be sure, if he is there, he will see you. Satan is one of those unseen entities behind the scene.

When the Lord asked him about Job, Satan did not hesitate to answer. Satan was familiar with Job. Satan had encountered Job in his walks back and forth on the earth. From Satan's answer, it appears he had scoped Job out. He knew about the hedge. He knew about his blessings and prosperity. Satan had probably checked to see what he could do in Job's life but was stopped by the hedge God had placed around him.

I think it is very important to see that God was the one that initiated the exchange. In actuality, God was bragging on Job. God was the one who asked Satan if he had considered Job and how he was blameless, upright, feared God and turned away from evil.

In this race, fight or whatever we want to call it, it appears to be important what kind of life we live before the unseen world. We give God bragging rights when we are blameless, are upright, are God-fearing and reject evil. Could there be some kind of challenge/contest going on between God and Satan in which we are players? I think so. That's why if we really understood things from God's perspective, we would know that it is not about us.

Now Satan's response to God's bragging was essentially, "The only reason Job fears you is because you are so good to him. He doesn't fear you because you are God. He's getting too much out of this not to fear you. Take away his blessings and he'll curse you to your face."

Wow. That's a serious charge. The battle is on now. First, God bragged on Job. "Look at Job, a human being on earth who fears me and doesn't have anything to do with you (evil). He's blameless and upright." It almost appears that maybe they had had this discussion before. Maybe Satan had challenged God that no human being would ever be blameless, upright, God-fearing and would also shun evil. God had to show him, "Look at Job. It's happening right there."

Satan has a comeback. Satan insists Job is the way he is because of all the positive benefits he's receiving from God. Now, with God being God and good and all of that, it follows suit that if you're in good with him (you know, living an upright life of obedience and trust) your life will be blessed. It's par for the course. But for Job, his blessings were a side benefit, not the reason for serving God.

TAKING GOD OUT OF YOUR BOX

For Job, it wasn't about his comfort level and having a good life. That was good, but he loved and served God for other reasons. God may have been assured that Job was not in with him for the money, but the only way to prove it was to allow Satan to take everything from him. You have to remember that, though God was the source of Job's blessings, Job wasn't living his life down here just to be blessed of God.

Be careful that you don't put God in a box, insisting on uninterrupted blessings. I have seen people get confused when their blessings are interrupted. That's because their focus has been self-centered—all about themselves. When we realize it's all about God, we can ride through temporary setbacks.

Knock, knock, knock. Let me out of here. Could someone please let me out of here? Most of us have God in a little box of our theological understanding. But God is much, much bigger than any box we could put him in. Even if the box was as big as the whole universe, he would still be bigger.

We trip when reality does not fit our view of God. We try to explain things away. No matter how you look at it, I believe it's clear that God was a part of Job's pain. At the very least, he had to give Satan approval to cause the loss. Now, that shatters a few theological boxes. But God didn't want to be in that box anyway, so we might as well let him out.

We can conceivably suffer the loss of everything and still refuse to curse God—that is, if we know it's not about us and our stuff. Perhaps you can look back on a time when you got out of sorts with God because he "allowed" something to happen to you that you didn't think should happen to a child of God. I know I've done that. Go ahead and admit how self-centered and self-focused you were at the time. Confessing our sins is good (Proverbs 28:13).

Let's look at how God answered the accusation that Job served him only because of the benefits or what he could get out of God. God essentially said, "Okay. You can touch all that he has; just don't touch him."

First of all, I just want to say that it would be a great honor to have God brag on me, but I've already asked him not to do so if he ever has a reason to. "You don't have to brag on me, Lord." Seriously, I'm okay with the idea, just not really thrilled. But I have said to the Lord that he has my permission to do whatever he wants to with my life. If that is part of the plan, so be it.

But I am encouraged by what I see here. Whatever Satan does in my life has to come through God's desk and be signed off on by God. Although I'm not too sure I would want God to sign off in my life on what he did in Job's, it is still reassuring to know that Satan could not just do whatever he wanted to with Job, a God-fearing, blameless, upright man who shunned evil. It might have been a different story if Job welcomed evil. Maybe he would not have had the same hedge around his life. Perhaps that would have given place to the enemy.

Of course, being bragged on is not the only reason we may go through loss and pain. Many times we open the door to evil. We invite evil in by murmuring and complaining (1 Corinthians 10:10). We invite evil in by our sins. We can also invite evil by the things we say. In fact, some claim that Job did invite "bad" into his life by stating, "The thing I greatly feared has come upon me" (Job 3:25). That may be the case, but I don't think so myself because it also says, "Job did not sin with his lips" (Job 2:10). But if that helps you keep God in your box, by all means, go for it. Don't let me be the one to cause you to question what you've been taught. God forbid.

Now, I'm not saying I'm at the place where God would brag on me, but at least I have a goal to work toward. And since Job achieved this in a time when the Holy Spirit was not freely given as he is today, I would suspect that, by God's grace and help, to become blameless, God-fearing, upright and to shun evil is even more possible for me. I also believe that giving my life unconditionally over to God means that Satan has to come through God before he can get to me.

The other reassuring thing that we find here is that God sets limits on how far Satan can go. Satan was told what he could touch and what he couldn't touch. Now even though I'm not volunteering to be placed on the bragging block, it is still good to know that Satan not only has to get permission to get at me, but he is also given limits when it concerns me. I belong to God. I am not my own. That's why I can look at life and know that even with things happening all around me, it's not about me.

FROM GOD'S POINT OF VIEW

Now let's look at this from God's perspective. His line of thought could have been: "Job has not done anything to deserve what Satan is capable of doing. But I'm God. I knew Satan would challenge me this way when I brought Job to his attention. But I know Job well enough to know that his fear of me is not based on what I do for him. That's why I picked Job and pointed him out to Satan. I wanted to prove to Satan that Job and I have been in relationship long enough that even if I withheld my blessing from him for a temporary period, Job would still know that I am God. He wouldn't be moved by the circumstances. He would know he could trust me even if he did not understand what's going on up here behind the scene. He'll have some doubts and questions, but he won't curse me to my face. I know Job. He knows me. We're tight. For a period of time, he'll probably have some problems with me, but in the end, I will vindicate myself."

As a result of God's faith in Job and God's confidence in himself, he let Satan go to it. All of Job's seven sons and daughters were killed, and he lost all of his possessions. But still Job didn't curse God.

Then Job arose, tore his robe, and shaved his head; and he fell to the ground and worshiped. And he said:

"Naked I came from my mother's womb,
And naked shall I return there.
The LORD gave, and the LORD has taken away;
Blessed be the name of the LORD."

In all this Job did not sin nor charge God with wrong. (Job 1:20-22)

Job did not see the big picture until he came to the end of all the difficulties and had a chance to have a little talk with God. What Job found out was it wasn't about him. It was about a point God was making to the devil.

Because we spend all of our lives in this natural realm, not many of us really think about the unseen realm. That's why it is so common for us to think about everything that happens to us from a self-centered perspective. But what we see and think on the surface is not all there is. Could God use your life to say something to the devil?

14

Living Down Here with Satan

It's a given that God is good. He is the author of every good gift and every perfect gift that comes from above (James 1:17). We also recognize that there is, unseen behind the seen, an invisible world just as real as what you can touch and see.

It has also been established that there are other spiritual beings behind the scenes that are not on God's side. These evil forces in the unseen world are behind all evil on this earth. Even though we don't want to put too much emphasis on this evil unseen force, we see from the account of Job that the earth is a place where Satan is still running to and forth looking to accuse God and mess up God's plan.

Satan is behind the "bad" things that are happening. I think it would be safe to say that if it wasn't for the enemy, we would not have bad things happening here on the earth. If we were all in heaven with God and Satan was already in the pit, things would be different. In fact, in Revelation the description of heaven tells us what we can look forward to. "And God will wipe away every tear from their eyes; there shall be no more death, nor sorrow, nor crying. There shall be no more pain, for the former things have passed away" (Revelation 21:4).

The question is not whether there is evil on the earth; the question is, can God use the evil that comes from Satan? As long as we are living down here with Satan, is it possible God can use the faithfulness of his own people in the midst of evil to speak to the unseen world?

Even though "bad" happened to Job, God had to sign off on it. When

disappointing things happen to me, sometimes I find it difficult to understand how God could even be remotely involved in it. I know God
is good. I know intellectually that this is temporary pain. I also know
there may be purposes behind the scene. But, I must confess, it still
messes with my mind.

I'm not the only person who has problems with the idea that God
signs off on bad things. I remember a lady in a class I was teaching who
just could not accept the fact that God has anything to do with "bad,"
not even by signing off on it. Her premise was that bad happens to us
because of the things we do to invite it. She believed we reap what we
sow and all bad comes from Satan, and whatever bad that happens to us
comes because of choices we make.

For the most part, I believe that is true. Much that happens to us is the
result of not following God's commands. His commands are protection
for us. They keep us close to him and shield us from evil. Some evil is just
the result of mistakes we make. I believe when we experience evil, we
should ask ourselves if we have inadvertently given place to the enemy.

But I believe there are some cases, rare though they may be, in which
"bad" may come into our lives just because God wants to make a statement to the enemy. That was the case with Job. That may be hard for
us to swallow.

Most of us probably don't live lives that are as exemplary as Job's.
However, under the new covenant, we have the righteousness of Jesus
in our lives. Jesus sacrificed his life that our lives may be lived no more
to please ourselves, but to please him. If we have truly given our lives to
him, our lives are not our own. We have been bought with a price. We
really shouldn't have major problems when things do not always go as
we want them to. We do not need to get bent out of shape when we
don't understand why we go through, unless we really haven't given our
lives unconditionally over to God. God is big enough.

I do not want to deny anyone's experience of God. It's just that each
of us has to realize our experience of God is limited. Someone else may
have experienced God in a way that is opposite of how you have experienced him. That does not make your or their experience invalid. They
are experiences of different aspects of God. God is so big, none of us can
experience all aspects of his being.

I remember a tract I read years ago that was designed for witnessing to an atheist. A circle was drawn. This circle would represent all the knowledge in the world. The person would be asked to draw a smaller circle within the larger one to represent the amount of knowledge he or she thought they had compared to all knowledge. After the person drew their circle, they were asked if it would be possible that God existed in the knowledge that was outside of his or her current knowledge. Likewise, to limit God to our experience of him, no matter how valid that experience may be, is still not the sum total of God. That's why it's important we don't keep God in the box of our own understanding and experience.

I fear many come to God under the false claims that having God in their lives will make life a bed of roses. We often are invited to come to God with the premise that it is about us. It is not about us. We get to participate with God in his plans. It has always been about Jesus. Our part in the plan will help God in proving some things in the spiritual arena. The only time it is about us in our walk with God is when we are spiritual babies.

A Christian who is self-centered and focused on what they can get out of God and their relationship with him is either a baby or an immature Christian. I am not in any way suggesting that God does not take care of what belongs to him. Nor am I saying that we should not ask for or expect physical blessings in our physical lives. What I am saying is that we are not to center our focus on our comfort, prosperity or possessions.

God's focus in life is not to heal us. I believe in healing. I have been healed several times by the power of God. We cannot ignore the time and attention Jesus gave to healing people in the Gospels. God's focus is to honor his Son. If healing an individual will bring honor to Jesus, God will do that. But it is not the end of the matter; instead it's the means to the end. At the same time, in some lives Jesus can be honored by faithfulness, perseverance and peace while suffering an ailment in a person's physical body.

SICKNESS AND HEALTH

We're not in heaven yet. We still live on this earth. Man welcomed evil into the earth by choosing the knowledge of good and evil. So we have sickness. Even though Jesus came to reverse the curse and made healing the children's bread, God's children still get sick (Mark 7:27).

It's okay to ask for God to heal us (James 5:16). Jesus destroyed the works of the devil by healing the sick (Matthew 8:16-17). It should be clear that God gives life and that sickness is from the devil. It is also clear that healing the sick is a way God overcomes the damage of the enemy.

With all we know about sickness and healing, is there still a possibility God can allow Satan to touch our bodies for a higher purpose? Many will adamantly say that is not the case. Others passively let Satan do whatever he wants, saying it has to be the Lord's will or it wouldn't happen. Each has God in their box. I say, let God out of your box. God is much bigger than your box, your own experience.

JOB'S BODY WAS TOUCHED

Satan thought Job was going to curse God when he touched his possessions and killed all of his children, but Job did not. In Job 2, we see somewhat of a repeat of what we saw in the meeting in chapter 1 between God and Satan over Job. Only this time, Satan came back and said, "Well, you know if you just touch his body, anybody would curse you if you mess with their body." And then God said, "Okay. You do that too." God granted him permission to do so but restricted him from killing Job.

> So Satan went out from the presence of the LORD, and struck Job with painful boils from the sole of his foot to the crown of his head. And he took for himself a potsherd with which to scrape himself while he sat in the midst of the ashes.
>
> Then his wife said to him, "Do you still hold fast to your integrity? Curse God and die!" But he said to her, "You speak as one of the foolish women speaks. Shall we indeed accept good from God, and shall we not accept adversity?" In all this Job did not sin with his lips. (Job 2:7-10)

A friend reminded me that one boil is very painful, but boils all over the body had to be excruciatingly painful. After going through the loss of everything, then to lose his health was more than a double blow for Job. Job had the wind knocked out of him. All he ever thought he knew about God was brought into question.

OUR ATTITUDE ABOUT ADVERSITY

Some think we can believe in God to escape adversity. God is truly a good God, and we can entrust our lives to him for care and protection. However, the first order of business is giving our all to God so his purposes can be fulfilled on the earth.

It certainly appears that God has a different perspective on suffering than we do. In fact, he promises Saul when he called him into service for him that he would suffer great things for his sake (Acts 9:16). Anybody claimed that promise lately? Stephen did not seem to have a whole lot of problems with being blessed with adversity. Stephen, a servant of God, was killed because of his belief in God. But even when he was being stoned, he did not back down (Acts 7:59-60). Stephen was typical of the believers in the New Testament. His life was not his own. He understood he had been bought with a price. Stephen ultimately gave his life up for God.

Not having problems with adversity was the norm for Christians in the first century. That's why, after the apostles had been beaten, they could rejoice that they had been counted worthy to suffer for Christ's sake (Acts 4:40-41). Contrast that with the prevailing attitude of Christians today. The Christians of that day had the attitude not of what they could get from God but of what they could give to God—even to the point of rejoicing in suffering. Like Stephen, their lives were not about their own agenda, they were truly committed to and available for however God could benefit.

Stephen did not consider his life or his comfort to be an exception in that commitment. He knew the years on this earth were small in comparison to eternity. He did not value his physical life over the purposes of God. This was Stephen's choice. Because he gave himself to God in this way, Stephen had a peculiar attitude while being stoned. First, he counted it a privilege. Second, he exercised forgiveness for his offenders.

WEALTH AND PROSPERITY

I hate to disappoint some, but the plan for wealth is not for every single member of God's body. While poverty is not a symbol of godliness, there are those whose calling in life is to give up material possessions for the sake of the kingdom (Luke 18:22). And there are those who God calls and gives power to get wealth (Deuteronomy 8:18). They usually also have a gift of giving. The purpose of their calling and gift is to benefit the kingdom of God and the body of Christ (2 Corinthians 8:14). When God gives wealth to them, they are responsible to God rather than looking at it from a self-centered perspective.

We've talked about Job in the Old Testament. He actually had both wealth and adversity. He also ended up with twice the wealth he had before his adversity. It isn't a question of whether or not God blesses with prosperity. He does do that. But we have seen he also blesses with adversity.

15

SPIRITUAL MATHEMATICS

Let's go back and look at Job again. God trusted Job to fear him in spite of what happened. God knew that eventually he would be vindicated. Job did not know the end from the beginning. But God did. When the whole event began in Job's life, God knew the end.

> For I am God, and there is no other;
> I am God, and there is none like Me,
> Declaring the end from the beginning,
> And from ancient times things that are not yet done,
> Saying, "My counsel shall stand,
> And I will do all My pleasure." (Isaiah 46:9-10)

Job was probably confused, wondering what he did to cause all this. Job's friends got involved. They gave him counsel. Even his wife told him to curse God and die. Of course, Satan wanted him to curse God and die. That was the whole point behind what had happened. On the other hand, God was banking on the fact that he would not curse him.

In the difficult situations in which we find ourselves, the odds are stacked against us to curse God and die spiritually. We don't necessarily verbally say, "God, I curse you because you let this happen to me." It is all in our emotions. We are messed up, wondering why all of this happened. If God is such a good God, why did he allow it to happen in the first place? As we continue in that way of thinking, our lives move away from being God-fearing.

In a class I was teaching, a woman admitted she had had a hard time understanding why her son was killed. During a police chase, her son was hit and killed. He was an innocent bystander. In the same class, another mother had lost two sons and was very angry with God as a result.

God knows who has a rift with him. Although many of us think we should not question God, I do not believe it is wrong to ask God questions. Even the "why" questions are okay for those who are young in the Lord. But eventually as we grow in the Lord, I think we need to change the kind of questions we ask him. We mentioned earlier we often ask "why" questions. An alternate question could be, "What point is this incident in my life making in that higher realm, that battle between God and his enemy? That was the answer to Job's questions about why he had to go through so much. We need to change our "why" questions to "what" questions.

Job had plenty of questions, but when God showed up as recorded in chapter 38, he essentially said, "Look I've got a few questions for you. Where were you when I created the universe? Did I seek your counsel?" Job 38:1-2 says, "Then the Lord answered Job out of the whirlwind, and said: 'Who is this who darkens counsel by words without knowledge?'" When God got through asking Job a few questions, Job's questions took on a different twist. They were not as glaring. When Job encountered God, his questions were not as relevant as he first thought.

An encounter with God made the difference. Nothing else changed. So ask God your questions and let him ask you a few questions. Get to know God. Let your encounter with him bring you to your spiritual senses. When we have an encounter with the God of the universe, we, too, will come to the same conclusion Job came to after his encounter:

> Then Job answered the LORD and said:
> "I know that You can do everything,
> And that no purpose of Yours can be withheld from You.
> You asked, 'Who is this who hides counsel without knowledge?'
> Therefore I have uttered what I did not understand,
> Things too wonderful for me, which I did not know.
> Listen, please, and let me speak;
> You said, 'I will question you, and you shall answer Me.'

"I have heard of You by the hearing of the ear,
But now my eye sees You.
Therefore I abhor myself,
And repent in dust and ashes." (Job 42:1-6)

GOD MAY BE TRUSTING YOU TOO

You know about Satan, but your problem is God. Where was he? Isn't he bigger than Satan? You know about Satan, but still God is supposed to be in control. He could've stopped the pain and abuse you suffered. That's a self-centered perspective. Let's look at this from God's perspective and see how much he trusted you.

When you get with God and talk things out, you might find out about God's incredible trust in you. You might even find out God allowed some stuff to happen because he trusted his care for you and trusted you would know how much he loves you. He trusted you to hang in there with him in the dark night of your soul. Even now when he thinks of you, he smiles and thinks this about you: *She's still going to love me. She's still going to fear me. I know that.* It does not matter that currently we may be off in the corner having a temper tantrum. I imagine God saying to himself: *I know her well enough. She knows I love her immensely. I sent my Son to die for her. She wouldn't allow anything to stop her from drawing close to me.*

When Satan does throw his best shot and we're thrown into a frenzy of not knowing what to do, at times, we do begin to draw away from God. Maybe we are not even aware that we have been holding back. We are still active in religious activities. No one else suspects we are not on speaking terms with God.

God just happened to think that you would know of his great love for you and that you would still draw close to him. He heard you say, "I surrender all." He just happened to believe that you meant that. If you lost your job, he did not think you would accuse him of being evil. He thought you had told him the job was his since he was the one who had given it to you.

God is grieved by this response to our loss. He really thought we meant it when we said *he* was the center of our joy. He didn't know we were talking about the job, our boyfriend or our children. When we said nothing meant more to us than pleasing him, he thought we meant it. Now we're running from him. Now we won't come close to God. We won't give God even a little time.

We don't commune with him like we used to. He misses us. We don't climb into his lap like we used to. God misses us. We show up in church because we don't want others to know we're at odds with God. While we've fooled everyone else, we know we have a rift with God. It's hard for us to admit that even to ourselves. We pretend everything is okay. "God, I still love you. I know we don't talk much. There really is nothing. It's just . . ."

But he still believes in us. He stands waiting for us to return. He hasn't given up. He knows one day we'll come to our senses and come home. He is looking in our direction every day, waiting for us to come home.

God loves you. That's a fact. God has proved his love beyond a shadow of a doubt by sending his Son to die for you. Nothing will erase that love. Nothing can separate you from his love. Nothing can take place in your life that will take away God's love from you. No matter how evil something is, it does not lessen God's love. Your bad circumstances cannot subtract God's love from you. That's the first rule in spiritual mathematics. You, plus or minus bad circumstances, equal God's love.

> Who shall separate us from the love of Christ? Shall tribulation, or distress, or persecution, or famine, or nakedness, or peril, or sword? As it is written:
>
>> "For Your sake we are killed all day long;
>> We are accounted as sheep for the slaughter."
>
> Yet in all these things we are more than conquerors through him who loved us. For I am persuaded that neither death nor life, nor angels nor principalities nor powers, nor things present nor things to come, nor height nor depth, nor any other created thing, shall be able to separate us from the love of God which is in Christ Jesus our Lord. (Romans 8:35-39)

Because he's God, he does things in a way that you would never do things. And you don't even have to understand how or why he does them that way. All you need to know is that God loves you, he cares for you, and nothing will separate you from his love.

That's why he tells you in everything to give thanks, for this is the will of God in Christ Jesus concerning you (1Thessalonians 5:18). Just give thanks. No matter what you're going through, find something to be thankful for. If your son gets in a fight at school, give thanks he hasn't dropped out of school. If he has dropped out of school, give thanks he hasn't dropped out of life.

That's why God tells you to "be anxious for nothing, but in everything with prayer and supplication, with thanksgiving, let your requests be made known to God; and the peace of God, which surpasses all understanding, will guard your hearts and minds through Christ Jesus" (Philippians 4:6).

God says, "If you allow me to, when I come close, I'll heal your wounds and hurts. I'll heal them all. I won't stop with healing, I'll fill those empty spaces with my presence and power. I'll restore what you lost. I'll give you a greater knowledge of me. Aren't I worth more to you than anything else?"

None of your problems will ever mean that he doesn't love you. There's not one problem, not one situation, not one trial you're going through that means God doesn't love you. Problems do not separate us from the love of God. Nothing can separate you from his love. He loves you. Take that as the truth.

THE GREAT TRASH RECYCLER

Not only does he love you, but God is a great trash recycler. No matter what kind of trash you have encountered in your life, God can recycle it. I often say, "God was the first trash recycler." All things can work together for good (Romans 8:28). I don't care how bad it is for you, it still can work together for good. God will allow Satan to put some trash on you, knowing that because he's God he can come from behind, clean up the trash, recycle the trash and make something better. The second rule in spiritual mathematics is that God plus bad circumstances equals good.

God is not upset about the stuff he's allowed Satan to do while we're living down here with Satan running about the earth. God is sovereign. He's God. Yes, he could have stopped it. But God's ways are higher.

"Satan knew I chose you. Satan tried to mess with my plan by causing you pain and abuse. He wanted you to turn away from me. But if you understand why I've chosen you, you'll stop listening to Satan's lies. You'll realize that, as you draw close to me and as I draw close to you, we'll get to be so tight that together we'll take care of the devil.

"You're mad. You're angry, right? You're angry because of all the stuff that happened? Okay. That's good. I need you to be angry; I need you to have a righteous indignation. I can't use someone who is passive. I need you to be good and mad. Look back at all the junk Satan has done in your life, your children's lives and your friend's life. Are you angry now? Good. Now that you understand where the junk came from, I can use your anger. Add my power to your anger and that will be a winning combination that'll keep the enemy running.

"Yeah, I allowed him to do some stuff to you. I purposely stood back and told him, 'Go for it.' Why? I knew for my purposes that I needed you to be angry enough that you would want to be in cahoots with me to go against him. I took a chance that once you understood what the enemy has done, you'd be angry at him. I knew it was a risk. I knew you would be angry with me, that you might not recover, and we might never get back to our good times.

"But I was willing to take that risk. I figured that eventually you would realize what the enemy has done. I was banking on the fact that once you became aware of how he's been behind it all, you would be so upset that you would be ready to volunteer for war in my army. You and I, along with all of the other women who see it from my perspective, will together put him out of business.

"That's how I recycle trash. I allowed it to happen for a purpose. I have a plan. What I have allowed to happen in your life has a higher purpose than just you."

God has chosen to use women to go after Satan. He put enmity between you and him. God is recruiting members for the WADD army: Women Against the Dirty Devil. How can he use an army that doesn't even care? How did Mother's Against Drunk Driving come about? They got mad about drunk drivers killing their sons and daughters. Once God gets some women up in here who are good and mad, Satan is in trouble.

There is an organization here in Detroit called Save Our Sons and Daughters (SOSAD), which was started by a woman who lost her son to violence. I also know a Christian lady who began a ministry of praying for the incarcerated after experiencing the incarceration of one of her sons. I know another person, Joe Williams, who founded and runs a ministry called Transition of Prisoners that helps former prisoners return to normal life. His passion for helping ex-prisoners came from his experience of being incarcerated years ago. You can read his story in his book *Sheep in Wolves' Clothing.*

There is something much larger than our small self-centered view of the world. Someone else is the center of all activity—God. God says "I am," and that's all that needs to be said. He absorbs anything added to him, good or evil, and remains God. That's the final rule of spiritual mathematics: Anything, good or bad, added to God equals only God.

As we conclude this chapter, let's review some things gleaned from the life of Job.

- God is good.
- Satan is allowed by God to bring "bad" into our lives if a good purpose results.
- God has to sign off on whatever Satan does to his chosen.
- God's goodness does not change when "bad" comes.
- "Bad" has a good purpose when it proves a point to the spirit world.
- Add a good God to a bad situation and good prevails.
- God is big enough and confident enough in himself that he waits to be vindicated.
- In heaven for all eternity, the "bad" will cease to happen.

When we look at these facts, it becomes more apparent that on this earth, in this space called time, the things that go on are not about us. That may not be a lot of consolation. But the good news is we will spend seventy years, give or take a few, down here on this earth but an eternity in heaven if we know Christ as our Savior.

In the meantime, let us agree to let God use our faithfulness to him in the midst of trials and even when we don't understand to say to the devil: "I believe in the goodness of God and count it a privilege to suffer for his sake. God is good all the time."

Part four

LIVING IT

16

WHAT DOES GOD GET OUT OF THIS?

Like Job, God may use our faithfulness in the midst of loss to speak to principalities and powers. But God often has more than one purpose to accomplish. Since we're living down here on this earth, let's see how we can think like God as we consider more of what God can get from us.

Trials are designed to show what's in you (Deuteronomy 8:2). If you've got the peace of God in you, if you've got the fear of God in you, that's what will show up in trials. But a whole bunch of other junk can show up too, if it's in you.

In reality if God is in us, there is no point for the junk. The junk is just a lie. It's a memory of the old that has already been rendered useless by Christ's crucifixion. But we've kept it stored in a closet just in case God proves not to be enough. For our good, God exposes the junk in our closet to allow us to voluntarily get rid of it. We realize it to be the junk it is in the light of the treasure he is.

We would rather not see what is really in us instead of embracing the trials and saying, "God, what are you trying to show me, what are you trying to develop in me?" Instead of embracing what God has allowed in our life, we run from it. When our thoughts about life are self-focused, everything is about us. We will forever try to figure things out. We will be upset with God. We will be frustrated. It's only when we look at pain from God's perspective that we can even begin to have peace.

We try to escape or numb pain. But that's leprosy, a disease that prevents a person from experiencing pain. At one time, doctors thought people with leprosy lost their fingers, toes and limbs as a direct result of the disease. But missionary doctor Paul Brand, coauthor of *The Gift of Pain*, made an important discovery while working with leprosy patients in India. He found that they lost fingers, toes and limbs because they could not feel pain. When they injured themselves, the absence of pain prevented them from caring for the wound, which progressed until it destroyed the surrounding tissue.

If you could not experience physical pain, you wouldn't know if you'd been seriously hurt. If a leper could feel the pain of a burn, bite or cut, he would recognize the seriousness of an injury and take care of his body. Instead the wound festers and grows, ultimately destroying an entire body part. Pain is a gift. It's a gift to show that something needs to be addressed.

The task is to draw close to God. Come close in the difficulties. It's in the fires and waters God promises to be with us (Isaiah 43:2). Part of his plan was to force us to get close. The fires force us to come close, and they also burn impurities off. The waters wash them away.

That's one of the ways of God that is not like our ways. God allows the fires and the waters to overwhelm us; he allows the flood to cause us to seek to know him. Many of us first came to God because of one difficulty or another. Many times we come to know him deeper when we are in over our head. Could God have had something to do with that difficulty? It brought us closer. It caused us to cry out to him. It got us to a place of letting go of the things that kept us from loving God with our all.

ANOTHER OBSTACLE IN THE WAY

Satan knows that African American women have to be close to God and that God will have to be close to them for God's plans against him to work. That's why Satan's main strategy now is to make sure we don't develop a close relationship with God.

Satan has to make sure that we have some hindrances, strongholds and lies going on in our mind that will keep us from being close to God. Satan does not care if we talk about God or are active in religious things. He wants to be sure you are not close to God and God is not close to you. He knows that when God is close to you and you are close to God he is defeated.

The devil is just on my back all of the time.

Oh, really? Why don't you get back in God's lap and turn to chase him away? This is a two-way street. Satan is your enemy, but you are his enemy too; and as long as you're running from him, you can't chase him.

When we wake up and find out who we are in God and the purposes God has called us to, we can stand in confidence in God and watch Satan flee. Now, if in our own strength we try to make Satan flee, it will not work. When we're in the flesh instead of being in God, we're in Satan's ball court. He's not going to flee when he has us on the run. But when we draw nigh to God, when we get all wrapped up, tied up and tangled up in Jesus, then when we resist the devil, Satan will flee from us.

We have to come close to the God of the whole universe. When we do, we have confidence that he is in us, through us, for us and with us, and we can turn around in his power and might saying, "Go away, leave me alone. And leave all my children alone. Leave all my friends alone. Leave my job alone. Leave my car alone. Leave my house alone. Go! Get out of here."

But try saying that when you're not close to God. Satan will look at you and chase you all over the place.

GETTING CLOSE TO GOD THROUGH CRISIS

Many have come to the Lord, gotten closer to the Lord or have returned to the Lord after going through a crisis. A lady that I met at women's retreat shared her life story with me. She was born out of wedlock to a sixteen-year-old young lady. The lady who initially raised her died when she was six years old. At that time, her grandparents on her father's side adopted her and her brother. She didn't have a good relationship with her grandmother. Her grandfather, with whom she did have a good relationship, died when she was in the tenth grade. She began to look for love in all the wrong places, never finding happiness.

Failed marriages, betrayal, adultery, chronic unemployment and bankruptcy were some of the things that led her to be fed up with life and ready to go to a Christian retreat when she was asked. As a result, she gave the control of her life back to the Lord and now knows that joy comes from a daily personal relationship with Christ, not from people or things.

Her testimony is God has been with her through the storm. She went through much but found God at the end of the trauma. Her life radiates the love of God. She is not down and out, but she is going through, now with God.

After one of my speaking engagements, I received a letter from a lady whose story shows how she came to God. This precious lady had suffered abuse in her marriage. Eventually she had left her husband and moved in with a boyfriend and had even followed him from her home state to the city and state where his family lived. In this new city, she was again betrayed. This boyfriend left her. She was so hurt; she cried and cried and eventually cried out to the Lord.

Out of her crisis she came to know the Lord. Now she is involved with a local church and, although she still struggles trying to adjust to a new city and raise her children by herself, she has seen the hand of God provide housing, transportation and Christian friends who have been helpful in getting her life anchored in God. Her life had been anchored in male relationships, but she now knows she has a purpose in God. She endured much pain as God worked in her life to bring her from the place of her former attachments to a place in which she is now free to discover her divine purpose.

This sister can now experience God's healing grace over all the hurt she has endured. She can afford to release forgiveness to the men who betrayed and abused her. She is determined to not let anything come between her and God's destiny. Some day she may even look back and be thankful that her boyfriend left her. After she has had a period of time under God's love and care, she may realize that if her boyfriend had not left, she may not have called out to God.

There have been times when I've gone through and have drawn closer to the Lord, but there also have been times when the pain caused me to draw back. Each time, it was my choice. You can chose closeness when you realize what you're going through is not about you.

WRONG THINKING ABOUT PAIN
CAN HINDER CLOSENESS

Another lady described the pain and hurt she had experienced in her marriage because of her husband's previous relationship. Her husband had two children before marrying her. Over the years, the children's mother had done things to make the relationship between the children and her and her husband very difficult. The two children are in their late teens and early twenties now, but both have distant relationships with their father. Her husband sometimes blames her. It is a very painful situation for her. She wants her husband to have a closer relationship with his children, but she does not know what she can do to help. She acknowledges that she reacted to many of the wrong things the children's mother had done in the past. She realizes she has played a part, but she knows it is not completely her fault. Because of what the mother had done in the past, this lady has to overcome bitterness.

If I talked to you in person, you probably could tell me of much pain, hurt and betrayal you have been through. It is hard for you to understand that God wants to use you. It is hard for you to see that God wants to bring you close by allowing you to go through the same things he has gone through. God has experienced betrayal, rejection, disrespect and pain. He identifies with you. You can identify with him.

IDENTIFYING WITH GOD THROUGH BETRAYAL, LOVE, FORGIVENESS AND LOSS

I remember a time that I was going through a misunderstanding with a friend. I was bellyaching with God over it, and he reminded me of how much misunderstanding he experiences with his own children. I was just getting a little glimpse of something that he goes through all of the time. We had something in common. I felt close to God. The misunderstanding was painful. But I got a chance to know God's emotion. God wants to use those who *know him* to do his exploits. So, was this about me or was it about coming closer to God?

God loves all people, even the people you find difficult. We judge people and evaluate them by how they affect us. God just loves everybody. He loves the person we are having issues with as much as he loves us. I don't know about you, but God doesn't get with me when I complain to him about another one of his children. In fact, he doesn't care for me speaking evil about anyone, even if they don't claim to be a child of his.

The word *curse* means evil speaking. It's a contradiction of the ways of God when we bless (speak well of) him with our tongues and use the same tongue to speak evil of someone he made (James 3:9-12). It's like you telling me that you like me but can't stand my son. Well, as far as I'm concerned, he's a part of me. If you can't stand him, then you really don't like me.

Because God loves all people, he might ask you to pray for someone who spitefully used you. When God first made that concept a part of my life, I was blown away. Someone had done something that really hurt me and God wanted me to pray for her? PLEEASE! I'll pray that a Mack truck'll hit her. No, I'm not that mean. A little Ford Ranger will do the job. Just kidding.

Anyway, I knew the Word about praying for those who spitefully use you but just hadn't been confronted with the opportunity to put it into practice. Here I was going through one of the most painful experiences I had ever had and God's ways were so different from mine. He even showed me that, if he wanted this person to have increased prayer, he has the prerogative to bring her into my life and have her spitefully use me so that she gets the extra prayer she needs. That is if I understand things from his perspective, knowing it's not about me.

It also means I have to be securely anchored in his incredible love for me. The more I see the extent he goes to show his love to another human through bringing "death" experiences in my life, the more I see how much it cost for his Son to die to purchase my freedom. In identifying with my elder brother, Jesus, I get closer to God. What an incredible way of doing things! His ways are not like mine.

Hmmm. I wonder if God would allow my husband to irritate me to get more prayer going up for him. If I really have it going on with the Lord, would God bring a person into my life who could use all this glorious prayer power? Would that mean the more prayer a person needs, the worse he or she may act up around us? Doesn't make much sense to me. I'm just wondering out loud. But you know what? I think I'll increase my prayer for my husband so we won't have to get to that.

Another time, I saw God's love for someone manifested at my expense. Well, I thought it was at my expense because I was looking at it selfishly. I've not always been open to having people get close. Because of having to leave many good friends when I moved from Chicago to Detroit, I was cautious about establishing new friends. I had made a few, but I was going really slow. I just don't like losing. My fear was getting close to people and then having to lose the relationships again. I just did not want that pain.

A lady accompanied me on a speaking engagement. We had a lot of time to talk driving from Detroit to Indianapolis. We really connected and before I knew it, we had become friends. It was almost as if she snuck over the walls I had placed around my life as far as friends were concerned. I really enjoyed the time of sharing. My thinking was stimulated by our conversations.

However, she was battling cancer. Of course, God knew it was an act of faith for me to allow someone to get so close in such a short period of time; surely this friendship would last a long time. God just had to heal her, or so I thought.

Well, she died. I was devastated and ticked off with God. I remember driving back from taking my children to school after learning of her death and crying my eyes out, letting the Lord know how cruel I thought he was to let me get close to someone when he knew she was going to die.

"Lord, you know I don't like losing. How could you do this to *me*? You can heal! Why didn't you heal her? It's your fault *I'm* going through this pain. You could have at least done what only you can do. You could have healed her! Why did *I* ever let someone get close like that? Now you know why *I* don't let people in my life. You just yank them out by moving me or letting them die. Forget it. *I'll* just go back to being a loner. *I* don't need people. This hurts too much, Lord. *I* can't believe you know what you're doing. If you knew you weren't going to heal her, then what was our friendship all about?"

"It wasn't about you."

"What do you mean, it wasn't about me? Of course it was about me. Finally, someone here in Detroit with whom I felt comfortable sharing my radical thinking. She didn't judge me if I didn't think on traditional lines. I felt so liberated talking to her. The conversations with her were reminiscent of ones I'd had with my good friend Brenda. You were the one who made us leave Chicago and all my good friends there to move here. Of course it's about me. I thought her friendship was your way of making it up to me for forcing me to leave Chicago."

"It wasn't about you."

"Then who in the world was it about?!"

"Maybe it was about Denise. She only had a few months left in this world, could I not have blessed my daughter with your friendship as a means of comfort?"

"I blessed her? Really, I hadn't thought of it that way. You mean she liked being friends with me too? I was just thinking . . ."

"I know. You were only thinking about what *you* were getting from it. But everything is not about you."

"I guess not. But still, why did you allow me to get so close to her and then just take her away?"

"Would you have rather not known her?"

"No, I didn't mean that. I just meant . . . why did you let it last such a short time?"

"If you were truly blessed by the relationship and your life was enriched by it, why are you not grateful that I allowed her to be in your life instead of bemoaning how short the time was? What if you had never connected? Look at that loss. I didn't have to bless you with her life. Be grateful."

"Oh. I see your point. That's a different way of looking at it."

"My ways are not yours."

Look at your past experiences and even your current situation in the light of what God is getting out of this. How is he changing me? Is he getting glory? Am I learning how to identify with the pain, betrayal or rejection he experiences?

It's not about you. It may be about someone else.

17

Putting On the Clothes of Humility

I f someone asked you to put on the clothes of humility, what would you do? How could you put on humility? Could you go to the store and pick up humility? Is humility ever on sale? Perhaps we can get it for a discount. Is humility costly? Well, we will shortly see that the price of humility is very high. Humility could cost us our very lives. Perhaps that is why so few people wear the clothes of humility. They just cost too much.

"I really like this outfit, but I'm going to have to come back. I don't have the means to purchase it right now."

Have you been putting off getting that new humility outfit because you didn't think you could afford it? Well, you can afford it. If you are in Christ, he already took care of the bill. Just go to heaven's market and pick up the garment. It has been tailored to fit you precisely. No need to go inside. The package is at the pickup counter around the back. It's been waiting there a long time.

The Scripture tells us how to be clothed with humility. "Likewise you younger people, submit yourselves to your elders. Yes, all of you be submissive to one another, and be clothed with humility" (1 Peter 5:5).

What does the word *submit* mean? We looked at this word very early in this book when we considered that we need to submit to God. According to *Webster's Dictionary*, it means to yield oneself to the authority or will of another; to surrender, to defer to or to consent to abide by the opinion or authority of another. Do you remember we said that to submit to God, we must surrender our way of doing things to his way?

When we think we should behave one way, we defer to his way.

Humility and submission go hand in hand. Yielding to another is a way of putting on humility. As we are yielded to one another, we are clothed with humility. So as you submit yourself to the elder as one who is younger, you are putting on humility. We've pointed out the following verse found in James before, but it is so important, let's look at it again.

Therefore He says:

"God resists the proud,
but gives grace to the humble."

Humble yourselves in the sight of the Lord, and He will lift you up. (James 4:6, 10)

Let's take a look at another place in which humility and submission are connected.

Let this mind be in you which was also in Christ Jesus, who, being in the form of God, did not consider it robbery to be equal with God, but made Himself of no reputation, taking the form of a bondservant, and coming in the likeness of men. And being found in appearance as a man, He humbled Himself and became obedient to the point of death, even the death of the cross. Therefore God also has highly exalted Him and given Him the name which is above every name. (Philippians 2:5-9)

JESUS GAVE US THE MODEL

Although Jesus was equal with God the Father, he took on the form of a bondservant. In taking on the form of a bondservant, he placed himself under God. He was equal, but placed himself under. Here we see the ways of God in opposition to the ways of this world. One would think that in order to be powerful he would need to take on the form of a ruler, not a bondservant. But the next verse describes how Jesus was able to take on the form of a bondservant: it was through the process of humbling himself. Once again, we see the connection between submitting ourselves and humility.

Let's be sure that we're putting on the right clothes. Is yielding to another really an act of humility? To whom is it most important to submit, and why?

ARE YOU ON GOD'S OPPOSING SIDE?

"God is opposed to the proud but gives grace to the humble." Okay, we do not want to be on any side that is opposing God. There's going to be a fight. On one side, we have God. I think I'd like to be on God's side. Let's see who is on the opposing team. The name on the uniform is PROUD. Who would ever try to come against God? Don't they know you can't win a fight with God? Like they say, "Your arms are too short to box with God."

Oh no, I just looked at the name on my uniform! The letters P-R-O-U-D are on both the front and back in neon colors. What will I do? I don't want to be on this team. I don't want God to oppose me. Let me put on a different uniform. Where is the locker room? I need to change clothes. I want to put on humility. I'm changing teams. I want God's grace on my life. I want God to be for me. I don't want to fight God. Who can I yield to?

"Submit therefore to God." Now it begins to get good. As we submit to God and take a stance of resistance to the devil, the devil runs away—he flees. I didn't want him around anyway. Good riddance. "Resist the devil, and he will flee from you" (James 4:7).

Since God is near the contrite and humble (Isaiah 57:15; 66:2; Psalm 34:18), it will be helpful if we have a greater understanding of humility.

So far, we've seen that we can put on humility by yielding to those who are older than we are in the Lord. We saw how Jesus, though equal with God, also demonstrated humility by making himself subservient to God the Father. We also have seen how we can receive the grace God has for the humble by submitting to God.

This is for everyone. Do you know anyone who does not need to be clothed in humility, be close to God, have God's grace on their life and have the devil running? I think everyone needs to hook into the humility/yielding connection. Every child of God needs to live close to God in his grace. We are in a fight with unseen evil forces. Our fight is not with people but with spiritual principalities (Ephesians 6:12).

Once we see the importance of this spiritual truth, I believe we will be running around looking for someone to yield ourselves to. Finding people to submit to should not be too difficult. God tells us in his Word different situations where it is appropriate to practice submission, thus clothing ourselves with humility.

We are told to submit ourselves to our government and its ordinances.

> Let every soul be subject to the governing authorities. For there is no authority except from God, and the authorities that exist are appointed by God. Therefore whoever resists the authority resists the ordinance of God, and those who resist will bring judgment on themselves. For rulers are not a terror to good works, but to evil. Do you want to be unafraid of the authority? Do what is good, and you will have praise from the same. For he is God's minister to you for good. But if you do evil, be afraid; for he does not bear the sword in vain; for he is God's minister, an avenger to execute wrath on him who practices evil. Therefore you must be subject, not only because of wrath but also for conscience' sake. (Romans 13:1-5)

> Therefore submit yourselves to every ordinance of man for the Lord's sake, whether to the king as supreme, or to governors, as to those who are sent by him for the punishment of evildoers and for the praise of those who do good. For this is the will of God, that by doing good you may put to silence the ignorance of foolish men — as free, yet not using liberty as a cloak for vice, but as bondservants of God. Honor all people. Love the brotherhood. Fear God. Honor the king. (1 Peter 2:13-17)

Children are to obey their parents (Ephesians 6:1). Servants are told to submit to their masters (v. 5). In this day, we would say, employees are to submit to their bosses.

> Servants, be submissive to your masters with all fear, not only to the good and gentle, but also to the harsh. For this is commendable, if because of conscience toward God one endures grief, suffering wrongfully. For what credit is it if, when you are beaten for your faults, you take it patiently? But when you do good and suffer, if you take it patiently, this is commendable before God. For to this you were called, because Christ also suffered for us, leaving us an example, that you should follow His steps:

"Who committed no sin,
Nor was deceit found in His mouth";

who, when He was reviled, did not revile in return; when He suf-fered, He did not threaten, but committed Himself to Him who judges righteously. (1 Peter 2:18-23)

SUBMISSION IS HARD

It's important to note that we are to follow the steps of Jesus by even sub-mitting to harsh bosses. Now, that's not too pleasant a task, is it? In fact, without the grace of God, it's impossible. Submission is hard enough. It will really take the grace of God to submit to a difficult person.

The Scripture also tells us to obey those who have rule over us in the kingdom of God. "Obey those who rule over you, and be submissive, for they watch out for your souls, as those who must give account. Let them do so with joy and not with grief, for that would be unprofitable for you" (Hebrews 13:17).

If you are young, find someone older in the Lord and put yourself un-der. Titus 2:4 tells older women to instruct the younger women. I have older women in my life to whom I can go to for counsel and prayer. Does submitting to or putting ourselves under an older person mean we allow that person to control us? No, I think it means we seek their advice on important issues and decisions.

In the multitude of counselors, there is safety (Proverbs 11:14). We're not talking about frivolous things, such as, "Should I buy this dress?" But certainly if you were contemplating marriage, this would be an in-stance to seek the counsel of those older than you.

I have sought the counsel of older women in the Lord when I have tough decisions to make regarding ministry. Every person should ask God to give him or her an older person in the Lord to be in his or her life. I have been blessed to have several. It really is a blessing.

Now, if you are employed, what does it mean to submit yourself to your employer? It would mean putting yourself under the regulations that govern your employment. If you receive a half hour for lunch and your boss wants you to take lunch at 11:30 when you would rather take it at 1:00, it means putting your desire under the desire of your employer. I'm not saying that you can't request a change if there is a legitimate reason to do so. But even in that, if the request were denied, you would follow the request without complaining and murmuring.

You might ask, "Where did that come from? They are just wrong to make me take lunch at a time I don't like. I'm sure going to say something." If you want to maintain the ways of God and keep free from the assaults of the enemy, you no longer have that prerogative. If we are to follow in the steps of Jesus, we have to remember to do it the way he did. He suffered wrong patiently. He did not revile in return. He committed no sin. There was no deceit found in his mouth. He did not threaten but committed himself to God, the righteous judge.

Furthermore, in the Philippians passage that speaks of Jesus submitting himself to God, we find that complaining and murmuring is prohibited.

> Therefore, my beloved, as you have always obeyed, not as in my presence only, but now much more in my absence, work out your own salvation with fear and trembling; for it is God who works in you both to will and to do for His good pleasure. Do all things without complaining and disputing, that you may become blameless and harmless, children of God without fault in the midst of a crooked and perverse generation, among whom you shine as lights in the world. (Philippians 2:12-15)

What if you are self-employed or do not work under a boss? We are all under the government and its ordinances. Yes, keeping the speed limit is a means of putting on humility. Paying your taxes, serving jury duty, following the posted hours of the city park, these all are ways you can humble yourself.

All of us have countless opportunities to put on the clothes of humility every day. Do you know that just letting someone in front of you in the traffic is an act of humility? We're saying, "You know what? I'm going to get where I'm going. God is taking care of me. I don't have to insist on having my way. Go ahead and take that spot. Have it your way. I count it a privilege to yield to you."

WIVES HAVE A GREATER PRIVILEGE

God has specifically given the responsibility to women in the home to submit to their husbands. Some would have us believe that men and women are to submit to each other equally. I disagree. I believe that women are given the greatest mandate for submission, especially in the home.

Others would have us believe that only the woman is to submit in a Christian marriage. The man is to always make the decisions by himself as he pleases, and the woman is to just submit to whatever he wants. I disagree with that view as well.

I guess you're asking, "Well, what do you believe?" I believe the Word teaches mutual submission in marriage, with an edge given to the woman because of her mandate to counteract pride. I believe a woman's submission has a purpose.

The Word of God instructs everyone to submit one to another. Husbands are also to submit to wives as instructed in the Ephesians passage. Yet, in two other places in the Word, wives are asked to submit to their husbands (1 Peter 3:1; Colossians 3:18). I believe wives have a greater mandate to be in submission. God specifically gave this task to women because he specifically gave women the task of defeating Satan. The reason God has singled out the married women for extra yielding is because of his purposes and plans, not because women are inferior or not smart enough. It was to bring his purpose of humility back to the earth.

If wives saw it that way, they would stop complaining. We would stop wondering, *Why did God do it this way?* As we see the purpose and understand the mystery, we'll finally get the real point, "It's not about me." Women will stop trying to wiggle their way out of the mandate when they realize the unseen implications.

In order for God to use us to defeat Satan, it is very important for us as women to know humility as a lifestyle. Submission and humility go together. The definition of submission is to willingly put oneself under. One of the reasons God asks the woman in the marriage to submit to her husband is because women especially need to walk in humility. If we are going to be the ones bringing defeat to Satan, we cannot afford to have any vestiges of pride in our lives.

Even if married women have a particular mandate to use humility against the enemy, that does not let men or women who are not married off the hook. Everybody can and should submit to one another. A godly man cannot biblically demand submission from his wife if he is unwilling to practice the same thing. Actually, men should not demand submission in any circumstance. In order for submission to be biblical, it has to be given voluntarily.

Submission is not about the husband getting his way. It's not about him. Why would he demand it? It is a privilege a woman has to bring defeat to the enemy. However, if she does it under obligation, she only gives place to bitterness and resentment, thereby nullifying the spiritual benefits. Submission should never be demanded. I seriously doubt whether anyone who benefits from being submitted to should ever bring up the subject by teaching others to submit or asking for submission. It is not about them.

Submission Is to Be Purposeful

Jesus put himself under his Father for a purpose. It was not just blind submission for the sake of giving his Father kicks for his ego. It was for a purpose of bringing defeat to principalities and powers. I believe a woman's submission in marriage should be purposeful as well. I do not believe God is asking women to blindly submit as a means of stroking a man's ego.

The reasons for the woman putting herself under are spiritual. Especially if her husband is not obeying the Word, she needs to put herself under. This will help him see what it means to obey the Word. I believe this is particularly true if her husband is not a Christian, but it can also apply if he has demonstrated that he is backslidden. I would call this purposeful submission.

The passage in 1 Peter 3 tells of this purposeful submission. Like the passage in Ephesians, it also targets women.

> Wives, likewise, be submissive to your own husbands, that even if some do not obey the word, they, without a word, may be won by the conduct of their wives, when they observe your chaste conduct accompanied by fear. Do not let your adornment be merely outward—arranging the hair, wearing gold, or putting on fine apparel—rather let it be the hidden person of the heart, with the incorruptible beauty of a gentle and quiet spirit, which is very precious in the sight of God. For in this manner, in former times,

the holy women who trusted in God also adorned themselves, being submissive to their own husbands, as Sarah obeyed Abraham, calling him lord, whose daughters you are if you do good and are not afraid with any terror. (1 Peter 3:1-6)

What would be some other purposes for submission? As stated before, one purpose for a woman to practice submission in marriage is to counteract pride in the individual woman's life. Since we cannot be women of pride and do the damage to the enemy that we are destined to do, I believe most of us need lots of lessons in humility.

There is no better way to practice humility than to do so in the marriage relationship. Again, we do not do it because we have to, or because we believe we are inferior or because we think submission is only for us because we are female; we do it for a purpose as Christ purposely put himself under. In our case, we do it so that God has a tool to deal with the pride in our lives and a way to demonstrate humility to unseen spiritual beings.

As stated earlier, if we understood the spiritual implications of humility, we would do much less complaining about the government, our bosses, church leaders, our husbands and our jobs. If we realized that the defiant attitudes manifested by murmuring and complaining were an open invitation to the enemy to come into our lives, we would not only change our attitudes, but we would be on the serious lookout for opportunities to put ourselves under someone else in order to learn humility.

If we understood that our acts of humility actually made a serious impact in the war between God and Satan, we would not concentrate on what we're getting out of it but on what God can get out of us.

18

Leave Adam Alone, He's Sleeping

Now, Rebecca, it appears you're saying God wants women to put on humility. I don't think women have a corner on pride. What about men?" Women always want to know, "What is God doing with the men?" When God begins to impress on us that he wants us to move on up in things of the Spirit, often the first question out of our mouths is, "What about Adam?"

When God would deal with me about confessing something I had done wrong to my husband, I would wonder why God did not use equal treatment. I experienced my husband's wrongdoings, and many times they were things that God would never let me get away with. Why was *I* always the one who had to admit my wrongdoings first? Why did it seem like *I* would always be the one who had to humble myself? Why was God always dealing with *my* attitudes? What about my Adam, my husband, Uwaifo?

I knew God wanted me to mature. But I thought that God should be just as interested in my husband maturing too. Besides, isn't the man supposed to be the spiritual leader?

Many of us, whether married or single, have bought into the lie that the family's spiritual life is dependent on a man, or the husband. When he is not doing the things we think a spiritual leader should do, we get frustrated. A single female parent will feel her family is at a disadvantage spiritually simply because there is no male Christian leader in the home. Because of this type of thinking, single women will often relentlessly judge a young man by impossible standards when considering marriage.

When I complained to God, saying, "Why me? God, why are you concentrating on me?" The Lord had to show me that there was a timing issue; this was God's time for me to concentrate on spiritual matters. There would also be a time for my husband to do so. I was confused because I thought God had the timing backward. "Shouldn't it be my husband's time first and then, through my husband's leadership, it would be my time?" This has certainly been the case for some husbands and wives. Perhaps your marriage has followed this pattern.

As our marriage deviated from what I thought was the set pattern, God took me down the road first. He specifically chose to work on my spiritual growth before he dealt with my husband's. I believe God works in a variety of ways. I'm sharing this with you not because he will always do it this way but because I think a significant number of women are confused like I was, and perhaps this will help them to get unstuck. God not only began to focus on me, he also told me, "Don't worry about your husband." You see, when we concentrate on others, we neglect what God is trying to do in and through us.

ADAM IS ASLEEP

Most women relate to a variety of men. In this chapter, we will use the term *Adam* to refer to the men in our lives. For some, Adam may be a husband; for others, he may be a son, father, brother, boss, pastor, co-worker or friend. Of course, some women have many Adams.

I was talking to a friend a few years ago. We were talking about men in general and husbands in particular. She was telling me some things about her husband. It was obvious she was frustrated. Out of that conversation, the Lord took me to Genesis 2 and essentially said that, in the period of time in which we are living right now, he has put Adam into a deep spiritual sleep while he is spiritually building the woman. Let's take a look at the passage.

> And the LORD God said, "It is not good that man should be alone;
> I will make him a helper comparable to him." Out of the ground
> the LORD God formed every beast of the field and every bird of

the air, and brought them to Adam to see what he would call them. And whatever Adam called each living creature, that was its name. So Adam gave names to all cattle, to the birds of the air, and to every beast of the field. But for Adam there was not found a helper comparable to him. And the LORD God caused a deep sleep to fall on Adam, and he slept; and He took one of his ribs, and closed up the flesh in its place. Then the rib which the LORD God had taken from man He made into a woman, and He brought her to the man. And Adam said:

> "This is now bone of my bones
> And flesh of my flesh;
> She shall be called Woman,
> Because she was taken out of Man."

Therefore a man shall leave his father and mother and be joined to his wife, and they shall become one flesh. And they were both naked, the man and his wife, and were not ashamed. (Genesis 2:18-25)

Adam was sleeping while God was building the woman. When God finished making the woman, he woke up Adam. When Adam awoke, he saw this woman, and he said, "Wow! This is flesh of my flesh and bone of my bone."

Most of us are frustrated because Adam is asleep. The enemy has used that to keep us from cooperating with the work that God is trying to do in our life. We are too focused on Adam. Again, Adam could be your husband, he could be your son, your boyfriend, your boss or your pastor. He could be your brother or brother-in-law. Any man that you are dealing with in your life who is not doing spiritually what you think he is supposed to be doing, he is your Adam.

I am not saying this will apply to everyone, but if this does apply to you, here is what God is saying about your Adam: "Let Adam sleep. Just leave him alone." Tell the Lord to continue his work on you. "Help me Lord, and work on me quickly Lord so you can wake up Adam. I'm going to cooperate now Lord because I don't want to be the cause of a delay in waking Adam up."

I'll say it again. It's not about you. It's about God's purposes to use women to bring defeat to Satan. You can be mad at God all you want. You can be mad at Adam all you want, but God is not going to wake Adam up until he's finished with you. God is saying, "I'm trying to build you. You're my woman. I want to use you. Don't get distracted by Adam's snoring. Adam is not only sleeping, he's in a deep sleep. That's what people do in deep sleep. It's your time. Look, everything that I've ever done is culminating right now in this period of time. You, as a woman, have come to the kingdom for such a time as this."

The bottom line is, "Leave Adam alone." I am not responsible for my husband's relationship with God. I can't fix or change my husband. I just need to leave him alone. When I focus on him, either in the spiritual arena or in practical physical matters, I have little energy to focus on what God is doing in my life.

The message God wants to speak to many of us is, "Leave Adam alone. You're the one I'm trying to work on right now. This is *your* time." Why is God's focus on us? His focus is on us because women are the ones that Satan has targeted. We are on God's side. God's focus is on us because we need to be very close to him to avoid the assault of the enemy on our lives. God is focused on women because women are God-ordained enemies of God's enemy.

Well, What About Adam?

Some may think that, by saying Adam is asleep, we are excusing men for being spiritually irresponsible. I don't think that was what God was trying to communicate to me. The intent of what God was saying had to do with the object of many women's energy and focus. I believe he was saying, "Get your eyes off of the men in your life. When you focus on them, it stops the progress of what I want to do in you. In fact, it's a clever little tactic of my enemy to keep you from getting to where I am destined to take you. I need your help. Right now you can help me by just leaving Adam alone. I'll take care of Adam. Can you trust me?"

Some men are irresponsible. In their spiritual sleep, many are messing up big time, and their actions affect all they are related to. It can really be difficult to not think about Adam when Adam is your husband and he is having an affair. If Adam is your boyfriend and he broke up with you after taking four years from your life, it's hard to stop focusing on Adam. It's almost impossible to not think about Adam if he's lazy, inconsiderate, mean, irresponsible with his money, and making bad career or investment choices. It's hard to take Adam out of your mind if he's your son and you see him making bad choices in his relationships. If Adam is your boss and you know twice as much as he does and you are doing the work while he gets the credit and twice the money, it will take the grace of God to get Adam out of your mind.

Does Adam's situation or his obvious wrong actions change the fact that God has work to do on us that is the focus of God's attention? No. In fact, Christina Dixon tells us in her book, *How to Respect an Irresponsible Man*, that God used the fire of her terrible situation with her husband whose irresponsibility caused them to lose a home, a business and much more.

Was it easy? Of course not. Did she want to bail out? Of course. But God dealt with her. There was much God wanted to do in her. When she finally settled down and let God cleanse her of the bitterness, anger and wrong attitudes, she experienced genuine heart-level change. Previously, she had been stuck on a merry-go-round of focusing on her husband's faults. After consistently applying God's instructions to get the log out of her own eye before attempting to remove her husband's splinter (Matthew 7:3), she saw her joy, her marriage and other aspects of her life restored.

"But Lord he's just not acting right. He ain't right. It's not fair for him to act up like that and nobody points it out to him. I know I'm not perfect, but I'm sure not acting up the way he is. Yet, you won't let me get away with half the stuff he's getting away with."

"Yeah, and mine calls himself a minister. Please! It's just not fair. If you want me to be a reflection of Christ, shouldn't he be one as well?"

Because many of us have not realized God put the Adams in our lives to sleep, we have been trying to wake them up—especially if it is very obvious that they are slipping spiritually. Some of us have been nagging them, trying to talk them into getting it right.

But God would say to us, "Forget about the men in your life. I put them in a deep sleep. When you're in a deep sleep, it doesn't matter who's talking to you, you won't hear them. So number one, shut up! Number two, stop worrying about Adam. It doesn't matter whether

Adam is your boss, your husband, your son or your pastor. Whoever Adam is, forget about him; he's asleep!"

When you're sleeping you really don't hear what people are saying to you and you can't see anything. It does not make sense to go to God complaining about Adam's lethargic spiritual life if God put Adam to sleep. Only God can wake him. God will not wake him before the time is right.

I am not excusing irresponsible behavior. It's just that it's not about your husband or any other man in your life being where you think he should be spiritually. God has a plan that is beyond you and him. It's not about you, and it's not about him. Chill.

God wants to build you up into being that Spirit-filled woman because he wants to bring you before Adam to show him what it looks like to be Spirit-filled and Spirit-led. Now, God is not going to wake Adam up if we still have a ways to go on our own spiritual building. Adam is not going to be excited about spiritual things if we only have one eye and no legs. God is going to keep Adam asleep until he finishes with us.

If Adam needs spiritual correction God can do that after he wakes him. Adam will be able to pick up things quickly when he has an example in front of him; he gets it by observing us. What took us years to learn through the study of the Word, listening to sermons and reading books, Adam can take one look at us and have it. God made us different in that way. God can then put the man and woman together to accomplish five times more than either of us could accomplish by ourselves. God is God. He can do things quickly when he determines it's necessary. Women, we just need to settle down and focus on God's ability to do exceedingly more than we can ask about or think. We need to trust God and just leave Adam alone.

I am not saying that in refusing to focus on Adam that we do not take certain actions such as confrontation, protection, prayer, police intervention and involvement, separation, reporting behavior, or anything else that God would lead us to do when we are facing matters of domestic violence, immorality, unemployment, financial irresponsibility, substance abuse and many other demonic traps that plague our urban areas. Obviously, women in relationship with men in these traps need the serious counsel of others and need to hear from God specifically for their situation.

Sometimes, we may have to create distance to get spiritual strength in order to deal with these demons. We may need to get out of the clutches of the demons for a while in order to get it together. There is nothing wrong with that as long as we see it as being temporary and for the purpose of bringing back reinforced strength and help to release the prisoners of war. Don't do it to cop out.

Now, let me make it clear that I am not advocating women marry men who are not Christians. That is being unequally yoked. The Word tells us clearly that we are not to be unequally yoked in marriage (2 Corinthians 6:14). But the Word also instructs those of us who are already married and have become unequally yoked not to seek to get out of the marriage because one of us became saved after marriage (1 Corinthians 7:11-16).

19

Does a Woman Need a Man to Lead Her?

I fear many women miss it when they think they have to have a man to lead them spiritually. When I was single, I pressed into God to the max. Granted, I did have an erroneous idea of the kind of man who would be able to "lead" me. If it wasn't for the divine manner in which God put my husband and me together, I would have definitely missed out on God's best for my life. Uwaifo did not meet the criteria I had set for what I thought a husband was to be for me.

What are the tasks for a husband in the marriage? Is the husband the person God speaks to and through? I believe some women want to relegate to their husbands the responsibility of hearing from God. Sometimes God speaks to the man first, and sometimes God speaks to the woman. The task in the Christian home is to walk in oneness and reflect Christ and the church.

God approached Mary before he spoke to Joseph (Luke 1:28). God told Abraham to listen to the advice of his wife (Genesis 21:12). God spoke to Hannah about her unborn child, and she was the one to relate the information to her husband (1 Samuel 1:17). Deborah called the general, Barak, to give him the plan of the Lord (Judges 4:6). Of course, many times we find God speaking to the man first; the point I'm making is that God does not necessarily do it one way all of the time.

When a woman thinks she is inferior to her husband, she will not cultivate a relationship with God that is truly her own. This is not how God designed the new covenant. Christ went to the cross and took our sin on himself to open up a new and living way for all people to relate to God without having to go through a human mediator. I do not believe husbands, pastors or any human being are to serve as mediators between another human and God. There is only one mediator between God and man, and that is Christ Jesus (1 Timothy 2:5). Perhaps brand new believers may need help in knowing when God is talking to them. But the ultimate goal, even for new believers, is that they would hear from God on their own.

It is imperative that we know that women are highly valued by God. They are not in any way inferior to men. They can hear from God all by themselves. Now, having said that, I do want to say that there are some tasks that God has given women that are of a different nature than some he has given men.

A Different Way of Thinking

Just recently, an article came out in *Time* magazine about the state of the African American female. A young lady that I have known for a long time wanted to talk with me about the article. She expressed some frustrations over the lack of eligible young men. This is a very talented young lady in her early thirties who has it going on with the Lord. I told her that I was beginning to question the idea that the man has to be on a higher spiritual plane than the woman in order for the marriage to be of God.

Earlier, we discussed God's definition of leadership. Now, I told you from the beginning that my thinking was a little unconventional. I also told you not to take my word for it.

I believe many women worry about Adam because they have expectations for Adam that not even God has. This worry has much to do with this whole idea of the husband being our spiritual leader. Let me give you a little of my personal experience to demonstrate how much futile time we spend worrying about our men. I spent a lot of wasted time being concerned about my husband because of wrong definitions of leadership and maturity.

When I used to worry about my husband's spiritual growth, I measured it one way. I measured it the way I was brought up: knowledge of the Word, time in prayer, family devotions and ability to expound on spiritual truths. I grew up in a Christian home, a missionary family. I was accustomed to seeing these kinds of attributes in my father. Trying to stay in my "place," I waited for my husband to do what I considered to be the "spiritual leadership" things.

In my younger days, I remember thinking that I would have to marry someone who had been a Christian longer than me if he were to be my spiritual leader. I just thought that was the way it was supposed to be. He would have to know more about the Word, have had many more spiritual experiences, know how to hear from God better, be a spiritual giant or at least be spiritually taller than me in order for him to be a leader over my life.

Now I am aware that my expectations of my husband were not the same as God's. My thoughts on my husband's maturity were based on verbal giftings. I admired and respected those who could talk a good spiritual "talk." I saw talk as being synonymous to walk. To me, spiritual talk meant a person had it going on with God. However, my husband was quiet and unassuming. I was looking at the outward appearance, but God looked at my husband's heart. I remember hearing a pastor's compliment to my husband as a "man of God." Because I was using another measuring tool, I wasn't looking at my husband as a "man of God."

When I began to measure the inward things of the heart instead of the outward appearances, God began to show me the giant my husband really was in his eyes. I know many men who know the Bible much better than my husband, Uwaifo, but I don't know of a better father than my husband has been to our children. I know many people who can talk about love, but I have seen my husband's love and patience with me in spite of my unloving attitudes, rebellious spirit, hurtful withdrawing and pride. God has used my husband as an instrument of loving me to wholeness.

In marriage, a husband and wife are one. There is no way that my close walk with God will not have a sanctifying effect on the one I am joined to. Or vice versa. I believe it is an open invitation to either partner in a marriage, or a potential relationship, to be the one who follows closely to the Lord and gives an example for the other to follow. It may switch back and forth throughout the duration of the relationship.

Bottom line: Women need to let go of unrealistic, ungodly expectations of men. Jesus is my shepherd, not my husband. Jesus is all I need, not my husband. Jesus is my daily bread, not my husband. Jesus is the way I hear from the Father. He is my mediator. Why would I put all those expectations and more on a mere human being?

WHAT ABOUT SPIRITUAL LEADERSHIP?

I'm sure that by now many of you are being mentally bombarded with all kinds of questions. Isn't the man supposed to lead? Shouldn't I marry a man who is more spiritually mature so that he can be an effective head of the household? I thought I was supposed to be taken care of, not the other way around!

To you I say, have you ever looked at leadership according to the Word of God and not the world?

When Jesus tackled this question of who was the greatest in the kingdom, he clearly defined greatness and leadership in a different way. The world defines leadership as being in charge, in controlling and lording over others. Well, that's also how many Christians think of leadership in the home and in the church. However in Matthew 20, Jesus defines leadership as serving.

> You know that the rulers of the Gentiles lord it over them, and those who are great exercise authority over them. Yet it shall not be so among you; but whoever desires to become great among you, let him be your servant. And whoever desires to be first among you, let him be your slave—just as the Son of Man did not come to be served, but to serve, and to give His life a ransom for many. (Matthew 20:25-28)

Here Jesus specifically says that the leader is to be a servant. When we think of leadership, we should no longer think of taking charge or controlling. That's the way of the world. In the kingdom, the greatest is to be the servant of all. The attitude of a leader is clearly evident in Paul's statement, "Imitate me, just as I also imitate Christ" (1 Corinthians 11:1).

Leading means going before to show what needs to be done. Issues of gender and spiritual maturity are not as important to God as we make them. There is no gender criteria for the one who goes ahead to show the way. If women are being asked to serve, then according to the ways of the kingdom, they are the greatest. Like Paul, they can say, "Follow me as I follow Christ's example of greatness." If you really want to get technical, biblically, women are invited to be spiritual leaders in the home—that is, if you define leadership God's way instead of the world's way.

Men do not have to be more spiritually mature than we are in order for us to be in relationship with them. God is interested in each of us following him. Since Calvary, each believer is a priest before God. Obviously, each of us needs others in our life to fully be all God wants. But we do not have to wait on the men in our life—be they husbands, brothers, pastors or fathers—before we're able to move on spiritually.

Does it really matter who has been a Christian longer in a Christian marriage? What are the purposes of God for a husband and wife? Could it be that a woman's close relationship to God is essential to the task that God has called her to in the home?

I am not against men being spiritually more mature than women. It just bothers me that some of us have stunted our growth saying, "I don't want to go too far and leave Adam." God is working hard trying to build us, and we want to draw back because we don't want to leave our husbands, pastors, boyfriends or eligible young men behind. We think that, because he is supposed to be more spiritual than us, we'd better not grow any more because we may become more spiritual than our Adam.

We think we'd be unequally yoked if we are more mature. That is hogwash. Where in the world did we get that? I don't see it anywhere in Scripture. The Lord never asked a woman to slow down her spiritual growth because of others—whether it was her husband, her boyfriend, her pastor or anyone. Rather, it appears he invites us to get closer to him so we might, by our chaste behavior, show our desire for purity and holiness (1 Peter 3:2).

WE HAVE WORK TO DO

God wants to do some powerful things through women, and we need to be as spiritually gifted and mature as possible. We need to be able to hear God for ourselves. The only challenge that different levels of maturity present in the male-female relationship is that the more mature one is expected to demonstrate Christian love and character more often and more consistently.

In addition, there is no point in trying to compare the level of spiritual maturity between a husband and wife. Each person is in a personal relationship with God. Each person stands individually before God. A husband does not have to be more spiritually mature in order to be a godly husband. Neither does the wife have to exceed her husband's spiritual maturity in order to be a godly wife. In fact, God says comparing ourselves with each other is unwise (1 Corinthians 10:13). That should not even be our concern. We each have tasks to do that are unique to us. In God's kingdom, there are no competitions or comparisons. As long as both partners in a marriage are in the Lord, there is no unequal yoke.

It does not matter who matures more or in what order, it just matters to God that all of us get there at some point. Whoever gets closer to God can sanctify the other by prayerfully being a direct and indirect influence that draws the other closer to God. In fact, it is not a gender issue; whoever knows the Lord sanctifies the other (1 Corinthians 7:12-16). This could be the husband or the wife.

Women, we have plenty of work to do in the kingdom. We are in a fight against principalities and powers; the more of God's strength we have, the better. We should be striving to become as spiritually mature as we can. Spiritual maturity does not mean taking control over other people. It means possessing more spiritual power to pray and bring down heaven to earth. Spiritual maturity gives us a greater sensitivity to hearing God and an increased hearing with God. Our closeness to God gives us the ability to successfully rule over evil principalities.

It was women that God declared to be a threat to the devil. In my opinion, we need to be as spiritually sensitive and powerful as we can. We have a work to do. The work God has for us will benefit everyone. We are not in this thing to compete with one another. It's not about us. It's about a plan that was in God's mind before the foundation of time. Before we were born he ordained works for us to do (Ephesians 2:10). It's not about us; it's about God's plan to finally put Satan where he belongs.

20

It's Time for Something New

This *is* the time for women. God has already indicated that in the last days he would pour out his Spirit on all flesh, and he specifically cited women (Joel 2:28). God periodically does new things (Isaiah 43:19). Jesus' death on the cross brought about an entirely new relationship for the people of God with the Father—one based on grace, not law. However, we find that the men and women who loved God at that time had a difficult time adjusting to the new. They were so used to the old (Acts 15).

This new thing includes women's elevation to God's intended place. This new thing includes even a wider demonstration of God's use of women to speak for him. This new thing defies the traditions of men that make the Word of God of no effect (Mark 7:13).

Though this may be contrary to our way of thinking, I believe God is concentrating the majority of his work on the woman. God's plan has always been to have women and men as partners. Men and women have either competed with each other or controlled each other, but rarely have they worked together as partners. The way God desires men and women to relate to each other will often defy our old way of thinking.

The idea to consider is that maybe, through her prayers, patience and forgiving spirit, God will use a woman to help her husband become all God wants him to be. This is not necessarily a nice thought when we think of marriage from a self-centered perspective. In fact, I believe many women miss their assignment in marriage because they don't consider God's perspective.

Other women will miss what God is doing with them in their marriage because they focus on being happy, not on maturing. When there are struggles in a marriage or any relationship, we often want to escape the struggle instead of finding out what God is doing to change us. Instead of asking "Why me, Lord?" we could ask, "Lord, how are you using this challenge to grow me up?" or "Lord, what are you trying to show me about your ability?" Again, when we cease from having a self-centered focus, a lot of other possibilities will open up in our lives to teach us what this Christian life is all about.

MAYBE GOD IS USING SOMEONE CLOSE TO YOU TO MATURE YOU

Because there are so many lies that hinder women from being free, God is being unrelenting in his quest to take us to a place of living in the Spirit. He's determined to bring us up to a higher place in him. God is convicting us and correcting us. It hurts. Sometimes God uses the people we are closest to in order to bring us up to spiritual maturity.

In relationships with our husband, friends, pastors, parents and bosses, many of us desire things that only God can give to us. Then we become disappointed with these people because they cannot meet the unfair expectations we have placed on them. God never intended for our husbands to be our everything. I don't care how many mountains he says are not high enough to keep him from you, no human being can be the knight in shining armor who meets all of your needs.

Yes, God can use the brother in many ways in our lives as a blessing. But let's keep the right perspective. God is the source; the brother is the tool. Let's not focus on the tool.

Even as God uses others to bless us, Satan uses them to hurt us. As long as we remember to not focus on the instrument but on the one behind the instrument, we can praise God for the good and rebuke the enemy for the bad. When we think it is all about us and have an incorrect focus on what life is all about, we will inevitably be frustrated with the people in our lives.

It doesn't seem fair, but sometimes it is our husband, boss, parents, boyfriend or even our best girlfriend who gives us the greatest opportunity to become bitter. Because they are close to us, the potential is greater for them to be used by the enemy to inflict pain on us. In some cases, the fact that we are different also offers opportunity for misunderstanding. On the other hand, God can also use those we care about and are close to as tools to force us to press into his strength and find his purposes.

LORD, FIX HIM

I wanted God to fix my husband in the areas that I thought he needed fixing so that my life could be a little more comfortable. I focused on those areas. But as I look back, the areas that I wanted my husband to change were not meant to be changed at that time. Again, there is a time and season for everything. If he had changed in some areas, I would not have grown in the areas that God wanted me to grow in.

For a long time, I wanted my husband to lighten up about wanting order in our home. As a creative, right-brain person, I am not always bothered by disorder. Most of you don't understand that concept. Papers can be all over the place and I can be in my element, writing. It doesn't keep me from doing what I need to do. I won't even notice the disorder until someone else invades my territory. Because I don't want them to see the disorder, I'll straighten up.

On the other hand, my husband likes total order. Our two styles clashed. He would be upset with me over my housekeeping skills. He would make comments attempting to help, but it would just make things worse. It was painful to me to have to admit I was not pleasing to my husband. It was painful to feel criticized. I took his comments as rejection, and I felt like I could never please him. I would be upset with him for being so picky.

I asked God to change him and wondered if he really meant to put us together. I even went as far as having a secret death wish so that he could marry someone who would be better in the area of housekeeping.

But God didn't change my husband; he still likes order and sees disorder in places that I don't see it. I look back now and realize God designed my husband to be the way he was in order to work some things out of me. He wanted to deal with my self-esteem and people-pleasing issues. He used my husband to deal with something much more serious—a matter of the heart that had eternal implications.

Some of you are probably thinking that I really got my act together about keeping this house in order. Actually, I have improved, but I am not Suzy Homemaker. My husband is not out there bragging about how well I keep house. He still gets irritated. But the change has come in another way. I'm not stressed out because I don't have everything together. I'm more relaxed over it. I do my best. I realize I probably will never fully please my husband in this respect, but I'm okay with it.

My focus is not on God getting him to relax or God getting him to help me. Nor am I trying to become the very best housekeeper in the world so my husband won't be upset with me. You see the real issue for me was trying to be perfect. I wanted to be the perfect wife. Not meeting my husband's expectations for housekeeping made me feel bad about myself. God wanted me to have my self-esteem based on the internals, not the externals. God wanted to get rid of my perfectionist tendency and the feeling of failure when I had to acknowledge imperfection. God wanted me to become more concerned with pleasing him than I was with pleasing my husband.

I'm not saying an orderly and clean house is not important, but there is more than one way to clean a house. Since that's not my strength, I could have hired someone else to do it, but I was bound and determined to prove that I was the perfect wife. As hard as I tried, it never worked; or if it worked, it didn't last.

God has called me to be his servant, and I cannot serve God while I still seek to please man (Galatians 1:10). If God had answered my prayer and made my husband more relaxed in this area, I would not have sought God in such a way that actually brought the more serious issue to the surface. That was what God was really after. You see I had elevated pleasing my husband over the desire to please God. That was wrong. I didn't know it until, as a result of crying out to God over the issue, God brought it to surface.

The point I want to make is that the primary issue was not about me becoming Suzy Homemaker or pleasing my husband. Both of those were worthy goals. But the clash between us was the irritant God used on me to keep me humble and crying out to him. This eventually created in me a greater God-dependency and caused me to take my husband out of the place God wanted to have in my life.

I have improved. And come to think about it, my husband is more relaxed over the housekeeping issue. But that did not happen until it became more important to me to please God than to please my husband.

ADAM NEEDS YOUR HELP

I have found there is a great need for adjustment in our thinking when it comes to relationships, particularly male-female relationships. But I believe these principles also apply to all kinds of relationships.

I present some ideas that will cause us to question some of the things we have traditionally been taught about Christian male-female relationships. There is a saying that the definition of insanity is doing things the same way and expecting different results. Well, my challenge to you is to rethink the role you think a man is supposed to play in your life.

When you think it's all about you, you'll miss a lot of what God is trying to do in your life and in the life of your husband, boyfriend or brother in Christ. You'll miss out on being the helper you are supposed to be in his life. When you think it is all about your happiness, you'll miss how the person who is different from you is part of God's purposes in changing you.

When God determined Adam couldn't make it by himself, he said, "Okay, we are going to give him some help. God saw Adam needed help, so Eve was created. The account in Genesis details what took place in the physical arena in the very beginning of time (Genesis 2:7, 21-22). We do not know how long it was between the time God created Adam and formed Eve, but we do know God did not make them at the same time. We also know they were not formed the same way. God formed Adam out of the dust of the ground, but he formed woman out of the side of man. Woman was to be man's helper.

Is it possible that we have based much of our behavior and thinking that relates to males and females on the traditions of men rather than on the Word of God? If so, we need to be liberated so that God's purposes will be fulfilled. We often see marriage for what we can get out of it, but what if it wasn't about you? What if God gave you an assignment to help a brother and that assignment was difficult?

"I know God does not want me to be miserable. The only way I could be happy in a marriage is to have a husband who knows the Bible better than I know it. And I sure don't want another job, thank you very much."

In considering marriage, maybe it's not all about what you can get out of the relationship. Maybe God wants you to put in before taking out. It's not about you anyway. The person God wants you to marry may not meet the expectation you had in your mind, so you miss him when God brings him around. It just might be God would want you to use all that spiritual power you say you have to pray for an immature Christian man.

"I'll pray for him, but I don't have to be married to him. PLEEASE! I've got to minister to the world."

After hearing me speak, a precious sister in the Lord shared with me that she was certain God had spoken to her that part of her assignment on earth was to love her husband unconditionally in a way he had not been loved before. This was her assignment to help. Prior to marriage, she had many expectations for a Christian husband. Many of them were self-focused. She says she has had to let many of those expectations go for the time being. Not that she doesn't believe they will eventually be fulfilled, but for now she knows she has to seek first the kingdom of God and his righteousness and expect all the things to be added later.

Women who know God's hand is on their lives for ministry do not need to look at ministry in the traditional way. Maybe, just maybe, the ministry God is calling many women to is to help those Adams in their lives who are messed up. Intercessory prayer, confrontation, unconditional love and modeling spiritual maturity could help some Adams.

From the very beginning of time, the man has needed help. Many men, including some in our pulpits, have no help from women because of our self-centered focus about the relationship—the "what's in it for me?" attitude. We rarely consider that maybe God brought these men into our lives so we could help them.

When we have our expectations centered on "what's in it for us?" we don't realize how God may want to use us to help them. When we're focused on what we want out of them and confused about what they are supposed to be to us, a true mess is in the making.

CHRISTIAN MEN NEED TO REALIZE IT'S NOT ABOUT THEM

The more I look at what the Word of God really says about males and females in a marriage relationship and the more I hear women talking about how their Christian husbands manipulate them, make unfair demands on them, have contempt and disdain for them, ignore them, emotionally trample them and even physically abuse them, I begin to see why the divorce rate in the church has surpassed that of the world. This is both serious and tragic. God is not honored when we bicker, fight, compete with and hurt each other. He is not honored when we are not one with each other.

I believe men who are not Christians sometimes treat women better because they don't have the baggage of off-centered teaching. I have come to the conclusion that the devil has had more input in the way Christian men treat women than God has. It is unfortunate. But it is true. Many women are getting sick of the ungodly way they are being treated by Christian men.

I really believe a lot of what has been interpreted from the Word about male-female relationships is partly from men who do not understand women—and some who actually hate women—and are frustrated with how we are different from them. I believe little of the interpretation comes from those who truly understand what it means to be a servant and sacrificially love their wives as Christ loved the church.

When you look at the passage where Paul talks about the marriage relationship in Ephesians 5, he repeatedly emphasizes the fact that the man needs to love his wife.

> Wives, submit to your own husbands, as to the Lord. For the husband is head of the wife, as also Christ is head of the church; and He is the Savior of the body. Therefore, just as the church is subject to Christ, so let the wives be to their own husbands in everything. Husbands, love your wives, just as Christ also loved the church and gave Himself for her, that He might sanctify and cleanse her with the washing of water by the word, that He might present her to Himself a glorious church, not having spot or wrinkle or any such thing, but that she should be holy and without blemish. So husbands ought to love their own wives as their own bodies; he who loves his wife loves himself. For no one ever hated

his own flesh, but nourishes and cherishes it, just as the Lord does the church. For we are members of His body, of His flesh and of His bones. "For this reason a man shall leave his father and mother and be joined to his wife, and the two shall become one flesh." This is a great mystery, but I speak concerning Christ and the church. Nevertheless let each one of you in particular so love his own wife as himself, and let the wife see that she respects her husband. (Ephesians 5:22-33)

Once, in the beginning of the passage, Paul says the wife is to submit to the husband, and at the end he tells her to respect her husband. But he kept hammering the man, "You got to love your wife." However, this mandate doesn't get that much attention when the marriage relationship is dealt with.

IT'S NOT ABOUT EITHER OF US

The main principle we see in this passage is that it's really not about me and it's not about my husband. It's about Christ and the church. My husband and I are just a representation of something much bigger. My husband and I are to visibly show something that is in the unseen realm. We're the seen scene that's to show something that is in the unseen. The whole thing is really about Christ and the church.

Knowing why God is so adamant about building us into Spirit-led, Spirit-filled women will help the process. But if we complain, try to figure out what's going on with Adam, try to compare ourselves or even get into pride because it's our time, we'll have to stay on the building block that much longer.

God's ways are not our ways. God's thoughts are not our thoughts. The difficult assignment given to women in a marriage has to do with something far beyond just the surface roles of men and women. In the area of male-female relationships and submission and authority, again, there are some scenes behind the seen.

Christian men and women have to understand that God wants us to be one. He has given each of us difficult assignments in the marriage relationship, but when we lean on him to carry them out, marriage becomes a representation of Christ and the church.

NATURALLY?

Our tendency is to look out for number one. It is not natural for us to entrust our lives into the hands of him who judges righteously. We've been hurt enough by those who are supposed to have our best interests at heart. As a result, we build up protective walls around our lives. Naturally, we develop insubordinate attitudes that are the opposite of how God would want us to act. Then we wonder why the devil is in our stuff so much and why God seems so far away.

We pride ourselves in being a bold, strong, take-no-mess kind of people, especially African American women. Compliant and meek are not words that would describe us. "Why, if we don't take up for ourselves, who will? If I don't watch out for me, no one else is going to." Well, as we've been saying all along, it's not about you.

I believe the reason we struggle so much in these areas is because we really do not know God. We know much more about God than we know *him*. If we really knew him, we would know he is able to not only protect us but keep us (Jude 24). We would know him as our shield. We would know him as our provider. We would know him as a strong tower. We would have no need to fear what man can do to us. But we don't get to know God by listening to sermons or reading books. We get to know God in the trenches of life, in those tough places of having to choose to do it God's way instead of doing it the way we are accustomed to doing it.

OR SUPERNATURALLY?

In honor, prefer one another (Romans 12:10). Esteem others better than yourself (Philippians 2:3). We are told to submit ourselves one to another (1 Peter 5:5). How can we afford not to stop being self-centered in light of the unseen spiritual implications?

God wants to wake up his chosen vessels, women who commit to giving up their natural strength. His chosen vessels are women who willingly go through the process of growing in grace and knowledge of the new and living way, Christ Jesus, the life on the inside of a child of God. Ephesians 5 exhorts us:

Awake, you who sleep,
Arise from the dead,

And Christ will give you light. (Ephesians 5:14)

It will take a supernatural awakening for each of us to consistently re-alize that there is an unseen realm. The things that take place in the seen have significance in the unseen. God is looking for co-laborers, women who will help him make a statement to the unseen evil world by taking our focus off of ourselves and by operating in ways that are op-posite of our natural ways. To be the woman God can use requires us to think like God and to come up to his ways, the way of humility instead of pride. Following these mandates is not natural but supernatural and possible with God.

I pray this book has awakened you to the reality that this business with God is serious. I pray that you are challenged to seek after God with your whole heart, holding nothing back. I pray you have experi-enced healing as you have read the words in this book, just as I have in writing them. I pray you find freedom that lasts.

What would please me the most is that after reading this book you, too, would wrestle with God in his Word. I pray that as you engage with God you will know him instead of what you've heard about him. I pray that you will get to know truth. I pray for your liberation. Yes, I pray you will be free at last—not because of what I've told you in this book but because you have decided you want freedom so badly you will do what-ever it takes to be free.

Jesus died that we might be free. Will you die to your former thoughts for the sake of freedom? Perhaps you are happy with the way things are. That's fine. Maybe you don't like the idea of upsetting the status quo. That's fine too. But if you want freedom, there will be a price. Just count the cost. I believe freedom is worth dying for.

God is using circumstances, time and growth to change me from thinking it's about me. I'm still on my way, just a little closer than that spring of my senior year of high school.

I invite you to join me. After all, it's not about you.

Recommended Reading

Bevere, John. *The Fear of the Lord: Discover the Key to Intimately Knowing God.* Orlando: Creation House, 1997.

Bilezikian, Gilbert. *Beyond Sex Roles: What the Bible Says About a Woman's Place in Church and Family.* Grand Rapids: Baker, 1985.

Brand, Paul, M.D., and Philip Yancey. *The Gift of Pain: Why We Hurt and What We Can Do About It.* Grand Rapids: Zondervan, 1993.

Bristow, John Temple. *What Paul Really Said About Women: An Apostle's Liberating Views on Equality in Marriage, Leadership and Love.* San Francisco: HarperCollins, 1988.

Dixon, Christina. *How to Respect an Irresponsible Man.* Farmington, Mich.: PriorityOne Publications, 2001.

Eldredge, John. *Wild at Heart: Discovering the Secret of a Man's Soul.* Nashville: Thomas Nelson, 2001.

Florence, Thomas. *Faith Flows in Ebony: The Memoirs of Thomas L. Florence.* Spring City, Tenn.: Cedine Ministries, 1999.

Gillham, Bill. *Lifetime Guarantee.* Rev. ed. Eugene, Ore.: Harvest House, 1993.

Gundry, Pat. *Heirs Together: Applying the Biblical Principle of Mutual Submission in Your Marriage.* Grand Rapids: Suitcase Books, 1999.

Krupp, Joanne. *Woman: God's Plan, Not Man's Tradition.* Salem, Ore.: Preparing the Way Publishers, 1999.

Lutzer, Erwin. *Failure: The Backdoor to Success.* Chicago: Moody Press, 1975.

Munroe, Myles. *Understanding the Purpose and Power of a Woman,* New Kensington, Penn.: Whitaker House, 2001.

Osaigbovo, Rebecca. *Chosen Vessels: Women of Color, Keys to Change.* Rev. ed. Downers Grove, Ill.: InterVarstiy Press, 2002.

―――. *Movin' On Up: A Woman's Guide Beyond Religion to Spirit Living.* Detroit: Dabar Publishing, 1997.

Reeder, Diane Proctor. *A Diary of Joseph: A Spiritual Journey Through Time.* Southfield, Mich.: Written Images, 2000.

Smith, Rhonda J. *Destroying the Myth of the Strong Black Woman.* Unpublished manuscript, 2002.

Sorge, Bob. *The Fire of Delayed Answers.* Canandaigua, N.Y.: Oasis House, 1997.

―――. *Pain, Perplexity, and Promotion: A Prophetic Interpretation of the Book of Job.* Lee's Summit, Mo.: Oasis House, 1999.

Thomas, Gary. *Sacred Marriage: What If God Designed Marriage to Make Us Holy More Than to Make Us Happy?* Grand Rapids: Zondervan, 2000.

Webb, William J. *Slaves, Women & Homosexuals: Exploring the Hermeneutics of Cultural Analysis.* Downers Grove, Ill.: InterVarsity Press, 2001.

Williams, Joseph. *Sheep in Wolves' Clothing: When the Actions of a Christian Turn Criminal.* Chicago: Lift Every Voice, 2000.

Acknowledgments

It is with much gratitude that I acknowledge several people who played major supporting roles in the birth of this book. To Andrew Le Peau, Cindy Bunch and Al Hsu of InterVarsity Press, thank you for putting your faith in me as one of your new authors and for the guidance along the way.

Uwaifo Osaigbovo, Victoria Johnson, Amanda Johnson, Lucille Stevenson, Gina Watson and Tabi Upton, thank you for reading the manuscript at different points and giving valuable feedback and encouragement.

Thank you, Diane Proctor Reeder, for allowing me to use two poems from your book A Diary of Joseph, and also for your content editing. You're the best.

I also want to acknowledge friends, acquaintances and all of the women who so willingly shared their stories with me with the unselfish desire to help other women.

More than anything, I am indebted to many for their prayers. I want to thank my prayer partner Clotee Ware, who faithfully called me every Monday morning to pray with me, interceding for each deadline, crunch and case of writer's block, and for praising God over each attainment. Thank you, Lisa Fort, for your prayer support at many critical junctures. There are many others, but I cannot name you all. Just know that I am grateful. I am aware of the abundant grace of God available to me through your prayers.

I also want to acknowledge my family, my brother, Tim Florence's family, Elois Freeman's family and Westwood Baptist as well as Cedine Ministries for helping make it possible for me to spend a week in a cottage, away from obligations and hindrances, to meet a writing deadline.

Of course, I cannot take for granted the grace my personal family members—Uwaifo, Esosa, Esohe, Mandy and Nosa—gave me at different times along the way. Thank you so very much for your patience and understanding.

I also appreciate family and friends who joined me in celebrating the manuscript's completion.

Last, I want to acknowledge the many groups who asked me to speak over the last few years, affording me the opportunity to study, personally grow and develop my thoughts. Though there were others, I want to specifically acknowledge those who invited me more than once during this period. Verna Holley and others of the United Conference for Women located in Michigan; Gloria Ward and the ladies' conference committee of Cedine Ministries in my hometown of Spring City, Tennessee; and Pastor Robert West, Sharon Guy and all of the wonderful folk from Lamar Terrace Baptist Church of Memphis, Tennessee, thank you.